WHAT WE DO IN THE SHALLOWS
Confessions of a feral fisherman

DAVE HITCHINS

While the events portrayed in this book all happened, some person and place names have been changed to protect the innocent.

ISBN: 978-1-3999-0833-7

Cover photo by: Dr Mark Hewat
Cover design & typesetting by: Cuppatwo & Owen Bailey

For my dad who made it all possible,
and in memory of my mum, who gave me
a love of both words and wandering.

CONTENTS

"Many men go fishing all of their lives without knowing that it is not fish they are after"

HENRY DAVID THOREAU

0 FOREWORD

Fe"ral\, a. [L. ferus. See Fierce.] (Bot. & Zo["o]l.) Wild; untamed; ferine; not domesticated; -- said of beasts, birds, plants and fly fisherman with no money and dreams of travel.

I am a dreamer. My school reports said so. "Unable to concentrate", "staring into space" and "can do better" are common phrases on the neatly written cards that my mother has kept all these years.

I blame trout.

I started fishing for them at the tender age of nine. I didn't start catching them until some time later, but it was still love from an early age. When I wasn't chasing them, I was thinking about them, reading about them, or making trout flies from whatever materials I could find. My sister's pet schnauzer had a lot to do with most of my early attempts at fly tying, being grey and doggy smelling.

Not a lot has changed. It has been a while since I shaved a schnauzer, but the love affair continues. Unfortunately, dreaming of clean water and high places will make no man rich, and I am certainly no exception. But somehow, since I first left my home in South Africa in 1998 aged 23, I have managed to fish some rather special places; dream locations that I had always thought were out of my reach. Patagonia, New Zealand and Scotland may conjure up images of wealthy fishermen, exorbitant guides and luxury lodges, but it doesn't have to be that way. I am living proof. You just need a little determination, a little luck and a very understanding girlfriend. Even then, I haven't done too badly with just the determination.

I didn't mean to write a book. I have written articles for fishing magazines for years, and because I didn't have much of value to say, they have generally been about the places I've visited on my travels. I would love to have stayed in those luxury lodges and I'm sure I would have caught a lot more fish if I'd had a guide every day – but I'm also sure I wouldn't have as many stories worth telling.

I was 'outed' a few years ago in Chile, when I bumped into a kindly English gentleman on a remote brown-trout stream. He invited me to join him for lunch; cold beer and fresh trout cooked by his guide on the stream bank. We got chatting and quickly worked out that the US$500 that he was paying per day was about the same as my budget for the month – and we were catching the same trout.

"I'll tell you what you are my son – you're a feral fisherman!" he said with a glint in his eye.

Feral maybe, fanatical certainly, but I am no expert. If you want to catch more fish, the best advice I can offer is to spend more time fishing! So this isn't a guide book, and I hope it isn't a 'look at how clever I am catching all these fish' sort of book. Take it with a pinch of salt, and if it inspires you to sell the family Volvo and chase your trouty dream, my lawyer assures me that your spouse can't sue me.

Dave Hitchins

1 EARLY DAYS

I grew up in the city, in the sprawling port of Durban on the tropical east coast of South Africa. It wasn't ideal trout habitat. To be honest, it wasn't ideal habitat for me, either. With my Celtic ancestry and fair complexion, the overriding memory that I have of my childhood is of being hot and uncomfortable.

It wasn't just me. It was a fairly regular occurrence at my junior school for kids to collapse from heat exhaustion when playing rugby or hockey in the so-called 'winter', when temperatures still hit the 30s and the humidity only backed off a little.

It was a funny place for a trout obsessive to start life, though I suppose that you get people from Holland that climb Everest, and people from Switzerland that win the America's Cup. The Japanese probably have a word for it – the urge to appropriate that which is denied us by the geography of our birth. It's the same urge that compels English girls to dye themselves orange in the depths of winter.

I found trout at an early age. My neighbour and school friend Mark Hewat had family that owned a dairy farm in the foothills of the Drakensberg (Dragon Mountains) – a verdant region of misty hills and frosty mornings. It was pure heaven for the nine-year-old me, and I used to live for the occasional weekend invitations. It was so different to my cosseted city life with the open space, animals, dangerous farm equipment – and trout. There was a river and a small lake both stocked with the sparkling creatures, and over a couple of years we progressed from trying to impale them with makeshift spears, to fishing for them with the ancient trout tackle that we found in a cupboard. I will never forget running my fingers along the worn old rod, where I could just make out the lettering 'House of Hardy' and thinking what a wonderful thing it was.

We were never successful with spear or rod and I think those early failures entrenched my enduring regard for the trout as a wise and near-mystical creature.

Back in the city, I turned to the sea for my kicks. It held fish, too, I discovered; none as wondrous as the trout, but they kept me busy, as did the waves and the other attractions of tropical beaches. Perhaps a bit worried that their son was becoming a beach bum, at age 14 my parents played straight into my hands and sent me to a rural boarding school in the Natal Midlands. It was a mile higher than Durban, about 10 degrees cooler, and right on the edge of the province's most fertile trouting region. Things were looking up.

A lot of the kids at my school were farmers' sons. They came from all over the country, from the local dairy farms, the sugar plantations of Zululand, and the huge cattle stations that bordered the frontier with Lesotho, where cattle rustlers made cross-border raids like in the old cowboy films.

I was in awe of these guys and immediately threw my lot in with them. They were tough and resourceful, they could make things and fix things, and most had been driving since they were tall enough to reach a tractor's clutch pedal. Most importantly, they loved the outdoors – to fish, shoot, and go climbing in the mountains. All the things that were foreign and alluring to me. For some reason they put up with me and my soft city ways, adopting me as a sort of mascot, I suppose.

On Sundays when there was no school, they would think nothing of throwing a few provisions in a backpack and setting off into the bush, ignoring fences and any concept of private property. We would go fish rivers and lakes up in the hills, on land that belonged to "a friend of their father's". If that was the case, I'm not sure why we had to hide in the grass when anyone passed by…

If we tired of catching fish, we would climb the fence of a not-very-nearby game reserve and spend the day stalking the wild animals, seeing how close we could get before they got wind of us and bolted. On one occasion, we had the bright idea of stripping down and covering ourselves with mud and leaves as camouflage. We were so focused on creeping up on a herd of zebra that we didn't notice the tourist bus full of pensioners gawping at us from across the clearing.

We were never completely sure if the reserve held anything too dangerous. We regularly saw rhino and buffalo, but because they couldn't climb trees, we treated them like big cows. There was a rumour that there were a few leopard about, but we never saw one, and any self-respecting leopard would have been long gone at the approach of a gaggle of boisterous, mud-caked boys.

I loved boarding school. I can't think of a better place to be between the ages of 13 and 17. The problem was that at the time, it was completely normal – we didn't know what the real world was like. From a fishing perspective, I have never had it better. Most of those amazing waters that we fished are still private or syndicated and tightly controlled. To get a chance to fish them again, I would have to become a stockbroker, or a poacher.

Oddly, considering our general disregard for rules, we were sticklers for fishing tradition and would never have dreamed of catching trout with worms or spinners. We fly fished, but our tactics were basic. We selected from a handful of flies, and they were all giant. The Mrs Simpson was a favourite, tied on long-shank size-six hooks. If we didn't catch on that, or on a big Woolly Bugger, then the fish were obviously off the feed. The funny thing is that, as far as I can remember, they seldom stopped feeding. I might be falling prey to the 'when I was young' reminisces of the old, but I am sure I used to catch a lot more fish before I discovered small imitative flies, matching the hatch, and the 'proper' way to catch trout.

If I had to bet on it, I would guess that it was mostly down to South African entomology. Excuse me getting scientific for a moment, but I suspect that, compared to the ecosystems of the famous trout waters of Europe, America and New Zealand, the aquatic life in South Africa is generally bigger and buggier. There are huge dragonfly nymphs, damsel nymphs and a wide variety of frogs, leeches and other large critters. I even caught a three-pound brown trout that had a small black snake in its gullet.

So, while they will also feed on the smaller nymphs and insects like their sophisticated foreign cousins, South African trout are probably a bit more programmed to pounce on the large and calorie-packed morsels that they regularly encounter. Like size-six Mrs Simpsons.

Fishing pressure may also play a part. South Africa is a dry country. You wouldn't guess it to look at the tourist brochures, but three-quarters of the land mass is classified arid or semi-arid. Because of this, every farmer builds a dam to use for irrigation during the dry winter months. These range in size from little ponds to huge expanses of water comparable to English reservoirs like Chew and Bewl. Flying over the Natal Midlands, you realise that there is literally a patchwork of trout habitat right across the province. Some of the fishing is controlled by clubs and syndicates, but the majority is private and lightly fished at most. Some of those lakes that we fished as youngsters may have only seen rods a couple of times a year. This meant that the fish grew big and stayed innocent, which is just the way I like them.

We caught some fantastic specimens. We mostly returned them, telling each other that they would be too heavy to carry back to school, but secretly realising that while poaching was a victimless crime, stock theft crossed the line of acceptability. We didn't own cameras, so there is no record to confirm just how big they were. That's probably for the best. In my memory they will remain colossal, and I quite like it that way.

With such a golden start to my fishing life, a worrying thought has occurred to me lately. What if my wanderlust of later years, my urge to seek out the best and biggest trout on the planet, to the detriment of my career, finances and personal relationships... what if it is all just a subconscious desire to regain the piscatorial nirvana that I knew as a child? And if you don't mind, I won't mention that thought again.

2 THE UNLUCKIEST FISHERMAN IN THE WORLD

On leaving boarding school I was consumed by life in the big city. It was an odd time. The 1990s were a tumultuous era of South Africa's history. Apartheid had finally crumbled and the country was making a difficult and sometimes bloody transition to democracy. I had my own problems. I was making a difficult transition from an institutional rural idyll of boys and cows, to one of unlimited freedom, freely available alcohol and sweet-smelling creatures with bumps on their chests.

It was enlightening, though. After 12 years of school history syllabuses designed under an apartheid government, I now discovered that my gut instinct had been right, that it was mostly a load of bollocks. We were taught a warped account of history that painted the South African nationalist government as the sole purveyors of truth and civilisation on the African continent, bringing light and salvation to the grateful savages.

We even got a day off school to celebrate the Day of the Vow, an important day for South Africans of Boer descent that commemorates the Battle of Blood River in 1838. This is when a force of about 500 Voortrekkers, armed to the teeth with modern rifles and cannons, annihilated an army of Zulus defending their ancestral homes with spears and shields made from animal skin. 3,000 Zulus died and not a single Boer.

Commemorating that day with a public holiday always seemed a bit insensitive to me. That would be like Australia celebrating the day that Europeans first landed on the continent, almost wiping out the ancient aboriginal culture with both bullet and disease. Actually, they still do that, don't they?

All this social and political upheaval was difficult, but the hardest thing about university, the factor that was most responsible for my awful exam results, was having to concentrate in lectures when there were actual real-life girls in the same class. After four years at a boys' boarding school, they were like aliens to me. Of course I had a mother, and also an older sister, but with me being a laat lammetjie she was quite a bit older and I can only really remember her arguing with my parents about her curfew, or locking herself in her bedroom for hours playing Wham! and Duran Duran very loudly. A couple of my friends had younger sisters, but they never had the same effect on me as these exotic goddesses that I now had to sit next to.

Trout were the last thing on my mind as for three years, I trampled the hackneyed path of the angry young man, spending more time upsetting my mother than anything else. I grew my hair, and a straggly beard that went weirdly ginger. I studied English Literature and Environmental Science and started to become the worst kind of knobhead student. I started saying 'man' at the end of sentences and created myself a ridiculous persona – part poet, environmental activist and grunge-music aficionado. In truth, it was all a thinly veiled attempt at making myself interesting to girls. I cringe when I think about it.

I think trout may have saved me from myself. Somewhere between all the late nights, and beers, and ladies of questionable virtue, I was invited by some similarly pretentious acquaintances to spend a weekend on a little farm in the mountains – to "commune with nature". I took a fly rod as an afterthought and thus my fate was sealed. While my ridiculous friends sat in fields, playing guitar and eating magic mushrooms, I crept off and found a beautiful small stream, lined with willow trees and populated by willing brown trout with astounding golden flanks and red spots. I returned home as the fisherman that, deep down, I guess I had been all along. This should have made my mother very happy, except that with every trip planned, every book read and every fly tied, I was another rung up towards a level of fanaticism, common to fly fishermen and bearded men that live in caves.

I was now faced with a set of problems previously alien to me. Apart from a drastic shortage of quality venues to fish, I had no one to go fishing with. My old fishing friend Mark Hewat had buggered off to Cape Town to study medicine and my farming buddies from school were scattered all over the country, working their family farms, in agricultural college, or in the army. Of my pseudo-hippy friends, not one would have known a trout if you had hit them over their shaggy heads with one.

The only solution was to attempt a bit of converting. The most likely candidate, who also happens to be one of my oldest and dearest friends, was an amiable chap by the name of Julian. An ex-provincial gymnast and all-round sportsman, he had chosen to reject physical activity and meander through an academic career, avoiding anything more strenuous than lifting a heavy philosophy textbook. I selected Kamberg as the venue for his baptism as it is was heavily stocked, and I remembered catching fish there as a kid when my technique more closely resembled seal clubbing. What better way to get a man keen than having a leaping rainbow on the end of his line?

The day before we left saw us in the road outside my house, casting barbless hooks at parked cars. To my joy and consternation, Julian very quickly developed a pretty little roll cast, something I have never been able to master. Early next morning, brimming with expectation, we headed for the hills and the start of our fishing relationship. If I had known then what I know now, I would have thought it symbolic that on the way we took a wrong turning in thick mist and almost had a head-on collision with a tractor. I say this because, over the years, I have discovered that Julian is the unluckiest fisherman in the world.

This isn't to say that he is a bad fisherman. In fact, he has taken to the sport faster than anyone I have ever seen. His misfortune, I believe, is far more sinister than merely not catching fish. It's as though there's a malicious gremlin that jumps on his back every time he walks out the door with a trout rod in his hand. It manifests itself in a variety of ways, usually affecting only Julian, but occasionally touching some of us unlucky enough to be in the vicinity. All that I am about to disclose is true, though if you still have doubts when I am through, just to be safe, keep clear of Julian when the trout are rising and there is lightning about.

The going was extremely slow that first weekend and everyone battled to find fish – everyone except my friend, that is. He hooked more fish than the rest of us put together and lost the lot. I even saw him get broken up by a fish that couldn't have been bigger than a pound. Late on the last day, he eventually got one on the bank. This was a fish to be paraded in front of the admiring womenfolk back home. As it was probably the first live trout that Julian had ever touched, he can be forgiven for not realising how slippery they can be. It goes without saying that the fish ended up back in the water and Julian returned home with an empty creel.

On our next outing, the gremlin was on top form. We fished at a friend's syndicate on the Loteni Road, on a beautiful but breezy day. With terrestrials of all shapes and sizes being blown onto the water, the fish came to our dry flies like lemmings, and we were into double figures before mid-morning. Julian, who only had a sinking line, did not fare as well. In fact, he didn't even get a take.

That afternoon, we moved to a larger lake where we all caught a few small fish, although the big ones that we knew were there failed to show. Eventually, the wind died completely and just before sunset there were some substantial-looking swirls off the dam wall. I kicked across in my float tube and Julian scrambled through the thick scrub to get into a good position.

What happened next, I will always remember. The fish seemed to be cruising along the dam wall, rising every few metres. I couldn't actually see them from my position on the water, but from the way my buddy was stalking through the brambles on the wall, I guessed that they were something to get excited about. The next rise was about halfway between us and Julian covered it with a classic cast, dropping his little fly just ahead of it. A second later there was a large splash, then a shout of exuberance, followed by a sickening cracking noise.

Then everything went quiet, the only clue to what had just happened being a small patch of bubbles bursting one by one on the lake's surface. On the bank, a broken man standing in a bramble bush with an equally broken rod.

From that point on, we began to expect calamity, and we were seldom disappointed. Sometimes it was just funny, like Julian's first experience in a float tube when he failed to notice the strap that is supposed to clip between the legs. If you've ever used a tube, you will know that one's first instinct on getting a take is to strike high and lean back. Coincidentally, this is also the best position for going straight through the hole. On other occasions, it was just plain dangerous.

It is difficult to forget the time we were fishing from a small boat on a big lake near Underberg when a gale force wind suddenly sprang up out of nowhere. Just as we started for the boathouse, Julian's reel began to scream and he was into his best-ever fish. Big fish are seldom stupid and it didn't take this one long to wrap itself around the anchor chain, which was dragging along the bottom. With waves slapping against the boat, Julian eventually got the mess of line, weed, anchor and trout alongside. With no anchor, the boat was blown straight down the dam and into a mini forest of tree stumps, against which waves were breaking quite spectacularly. Surprisingly, all parties survived with a minimum of damage – even the trout. This was granted a reprieve and released on the grounds that it had shown true valour by standing firm and not abandoning ship.

Julian had turned into an excellent fisherman and I was very sad when he announced that he was off to see the world for a couple of years. As a final fling, we packed the camping gear and headed into the mountains near Sani Pass for a weekend of fishing and talking bollocks for the last time in a while. We made camp and then headed down to the river. Prospects looked good when I had two fish landed and a couple lost within the first half hour. How wrong I was. For the rest of the afternoon, I didn't get another bite, and had to watch as my 'friend' caught fish after fish. Luckily for the local gene pool, Julian returns everything he catches. I had certainly been taught a serious lesson by my protégé.

Way after dark, exhausted but content, we made our way back to camp, one of us secretly wondering if perhaps the fishing gremlin had moved on to some other poor sod. But things didn't look quite right as we approached our tents. To our dismay, we discovered that some or other beastie had been through our gear, and had either eaten, shredded or slobbered on our food supplies. It obviously didn't have opposable thumbs because thankfully, the beers were intact.

Having not kept any fish, and being a good hour's drive from the nearest town, we had no other option than to get thoroughly drunk in an attempt to forget about our empty bellies. After the fifth can, it seemed like a good idea to hazard a few throws in the pool near the camp. Despite giggling like schoolgirls and making more commotion than a wildebeest in a jacuzzi, I actually had a fish leap out of the water after my fly and almost land on the bank. It unfortunately didn't connect, depriving me of a belated supper and a good story.

After a while, the glow of alcohol began to wear off and we trooped back to the fire, where Julian decided that he was hungry enough to eat slobbery food. I went to bed, leaving him to barbecue the rabies off the sausages. Time would tell whether or not he was successful, though knowing his luck, he would be howling at the next full moon.

3 THE MAGIC FLY AND OTHER FABLES

When I was about 22, I thought I had invented the perfect fly. As I tend to, I had got a bit obsessed with fly tying, consuming every book I could find on the subject, studying entomology and even reading scientific papers on the trout's sensory system and how they perceive the triggers that encourage them to feed. Not a huge surprise that I couldn't keep a girlfriend.

I literally tied thousands of flies. I experimented with materials, different tying techniques and copied imitative patterns that I found in American and British magazines. Without fail, none of my inventions worked anywhere near as well as the handful of South African stalwarts – the Mrs Simpson, the Woolly Worm and the Walker's Killer, usually in extra-large sizes. In retrospect, I shouldn't have been surprised that a fly tied to represent a diminutive Californian freshwater shrimp wouldn't work too well in a South African lake that had no similar species.

Around this time, my old friend Mark Hewat was about to become Dr Hewat and had come back to KwaZulu-Natal to do a final year's placement at a local hospital. He was a member of a syndicate that had a series of highly regarded lakes in the Dargle area. This really was a golden year and we fished together a lot, rekindling the competitive relationship that started when we were six, playing some game in the road outside our houses.

Now while I used tactics that I had read were effective, Mark used tactics which he had proven for himself. I like the story he tells of a trip he had to a famous lake in East Griqualand. The landowner looked over his shoulder while he was tackling up and sniggered at the measly little fly that he was tying on. He magnanimously offered one of his own extra-long shank Mrs Simpsons from his plus-sized fly box. With it, Mark improved on his personal best three times that weekend. Since then, he has been a convert to the 'big fly, big fish' theory, despite me quoting him everything from Walton to Borger with a bit of Sutcliffe in between.

Now I have always remained optimistic that the wealth of information that I have accumulated will one day stand me in good stead. I have visions of running into a hatch of some rare insect that I alone will recognise, whereafter the trout will rain down on me like some divine plague. Of course, I will be fishing alongside Mark, who will remain fishless. You may not be surprised to hear that it hasn't happened yet.

But back to my magic fly. I always tie at least two of any new fly, and this time was no exception. It was spawned when I was tying the night before a trip and was a bit short of materials. What started out as a standard Damsel Nymph ended up as a mutant with a marabou tail, olive palmered body and a red glass bead for a head. It was very scruffy and didn't look much like any living creature, but it just seemed right when I held it up to the light.

I wasn't in the best of moods when we arrived at the lake high up in the Kamberg valley. The farm manager assumed that we had a 4x4 when he said it was a 20-minute drive round the back of the mountain and up onto the plateau. An hour later, having left chunks of my car's undercarriage on the 'road', I was in no mood to assemble a tent. Leaving the others, I grumpily stalked off with my rod and found a spot where a feeder stream formed a mini delta as it merged with the lake in a series of deep channels. Sucking on my new fly to soak the marabou, I waded out, keeping an eye on the weed beds, which swayed gently in the almost imperceptible current. Worries of panel-beater's bills began to fade as I realised this was a super-prime spot. I put out a medium-length cast over the weed bed immediately in front of me and began a slow retrieve. Suddenly, there was a light pluck on the line. I kept up a slow retrieve and with the leader almost at the top eye, there was a strong pull and a plump rainbow leapt out of the water, landing in the weed right in front of me, showering me with icy water as it thrashed about. All I had to do was grab it and the shortest fight of my life was over.

Chuffed that I had broken my duck without disturbing the other residents, I put out a longer cast over the deeper water. After only two retrieves, a fish hit my fly hard, pulling off a couple of metres of line before everything went slack. Expecting the worst, I started stripping in to examine my tippet. Another fish had different ideas, and this time fly and line did part company. I had an attack of jelly fingers as I changed tippets and fumbled the remaining fly onto the end. Three more casts produced two more fish, which must have scared off the others because things went dead after that.

I waded ashore and walked around the lake to find my buddies, who were all fishing by this time. They hadn't caught a thing and looked a bit sceptical when I told them of my success. I wasn't exactly Mr Popular when my next cast produced the best fish of the trip from the deep water right under their noses. Unfortunately, the fly got a bit mangled in the process, although it still caught another fish with a missing hackle and half a tail.

I was dead keen to get back to my tying vice and in the following days, I must have tied 20 identical flies. A big cold front had moved through during the week and I heard that some roads in the mountains were closed by heavy snow. That wasn't going to stop me and I left before sunrise on Saturday morning and floored it up the N3 to Pietermaritzburg, where I dragged a very reluctant Julian from his warm bed and headed onwards to Underberg. I had recently joined the local fishing club there, which gave me access to about 20 lakes in the area. We chose one near the main road so that we wouldn't get the car caught in a snow drift and carried our gear down to the boat house.

I appreciate any chance to get away from the city, but that was one of the most glorious days I have ever seen. The Berg held a thick mantle of snow that was extra white under a great clear sky. The pine and fir trees almost seemed to glow, perhaps because they were the only trees that had survived the snowfall unscathed. We tackled up under one of them, enjoying the novelty of being in a winter wonderland.

I opened my fly box and surveyed the fuzzy green flies, taking up two whole rows. Then I slipped out onto the glassy water in my float tube, cosy in my neoprene waders that had cost half of my first month's salary from my new job. Julian took the boat, which was iced into the boat house and had to be smashed out with an oar. I was soon into fish and so was Julian, once I had reluctantly gifted him a couple of my flies. Damsel Nymphs are not supposed to be active in the depths of winter – but no one had told the trout that. They couldn't get enough of them, and I later found out that we broke the club record for the number of fish caught in one day from that lake. Most were wearing their brightest spawning ensemble and they were all healthy and fiery.

By 4pm, we had to reluctantly head home as Julian was working an evening shift at the Crossways Inn. I stopped off for a beer and caught the second half of the rugby test. The Boks won convincingly, with local boy Wayne Fyvie having a blinder of a debut. The celebrations were long and festive and I seem to remember spending some time in the pub garden trying to convince a country lass that it was me she wanted to marry, not Wayne Fyvie.

That's the best days fishing that I had ever had, although I might have disagreed when I woke up the next morning on Julian's sofa. There must have been something wrong with that one beer, because I had a splitting headache and couldn't remember how we got home.

I was convinced that I had invented a magic fly that no fish could resist. I wanted to prove it by catching a giant one, now. The next few weeks were a frustrating time as I had to endure a horrid spate of social events. My own sister refused to postpone her wedding, even after I explained the whole saga. Eventually, I had a spare weekend, so persuaded Mark to invite me to one of his syndicate lakes that was known for its very big fish. The whole syndicate was actually named after it. Old men in the local pub spoke reverently of trout as long as your leg that had been known to take ducklings off the surface as if they were grasshoppers. I was very excited at the prospect of catching one, but mostly I was excited about showing up my old fishing adversary with my magic fly.

With an icy wind and an angry dark sky, it was not the most pleasant day to be out. If neither of us had caught fish, I would have blamed the weather. As luck would have it, the fish were feeding avidly – locked into a selective rise to an insect that must have looked exactly like a four-inch, black Dog Nobbler with a tin head. Having no such monstrosity in my fly box, I had to let Mark do the fish catching while

I took care of the water flailing, tippet breaking and mud slipping. He caught eight to my nothing. The magic spell was broken.

I still fish the mongrel damsel fly occasionally; it is a decent enough fly and I've caught a fish or two on it, but it has never exhibited any magic properties again and I haven't tied another, which is the most damning evidence of its fall from grace. In retrospect, I am actually quite relieved. Fishing isn't supposed to be easy. Hard-won victories are the most satisfying, when you have been challenged and eventually triumphed after blood, sweat and tears.

I am reminded of a fable that I once read. It tells of an elderly fly fisherman who passes away after a long and sporting life. Having walked towards the light, he finds himself on the bank of a sparkling trout stream. With a split cane rod that he finds beside him, he starts casting to the trout that are rising lazily in the dimpled current. With every cast he hooks and lands a plump fish, each more beautiful than the last. After an hour of action, the fisherman notices a figure approaching him. It is the water keeper who confirms what the fisherman has begun to suspect. That he is indeed not in heaven, but in hell.

4 DESPERATE TIMES

In the mid 1990s, South Africa was a rapidly changing country, but not everyone was happy about it. A democratically elected government had taken control at last and had implemented a policy of affirmative action that incentivised companies to reserve jobs for previously disadvantaged sections of society. It was a small step towards resetting the imbalance that had seen most of the country's wealth and assets end up under the control of a relatively small and mostly pale group of people.

Life isn't always fair and sometimes innocent people have to pay for the actions of their ancestors. With less rosy job prospects, thousands of middle-class people left for Australia, New Zealand and Canada. In the face of economic uncertainty and an apparent 'brain drain', the currency weakened and dinner-table conversation across the land was preoccupied with talk of rising crime levels and concern for the country's future.

I didn't go to dinner parties, but even if I had, I wouldn't have paid much attention. It would take a lot more than a bit of crime to make me leave my beloved homeland. What really bothered me was that I wanted to go and catch huge trout in South America, and no matter how hard I saved, with every currency devaluation, my trip fund actually shrank in dollar terms.

How does the song go… something about the streets of London being paved with gold? I should have paid more attention. I resolved to spend a few months there, working hard until I had earned enough sterling for the fishing trip that I had dreamed about for years: four months overland from Argentina to Ecuador. I could then return to

South Africa and pick up where I left off, minus the itchy feet.

I reckoned I could put up with England for a year. I would never have dreamed of settling there with its awful weather, crowded transport system and all the scary-looking women that I saw on Top Of The Pops. A few months would be tough, but just about bearable.

My confidence was fuelled by friends who had scored ridiculously high-paying jobs in the banking and IT fields. Guys who I had always considered a bit dim were earning R300 and R400 an hour, and I was convinced that as soon as I touched down at Heathrow, the employment agencies would be queuing up for my services. What I didn't count on was the 400,000 other South Africans, Kiwis and Australians just as willing to exaggerate on their CVs.

After four months, I was still stuck in a crappy office job entering tiny figures into a never-ending spreadsheet, for just enough money to live on and have a beer on a Friday night. And remember that this was London, a place where when you walk into a pub, most of the money in your pocket mysteriously dissolves. I was starting to get desperate. I'd bought my plane ticket with my first month's salary, but the spending-money fund was looking very sad and my date of departure was getting nearer. The employment agency wasn't interested any more. I was placed and they had earned their commission.

An idea began to take hold, which had been in the back of my mind since I first realised that £6.50 an hour wasn't going to make me rich. I had heard about pharmaceutical drug trials and had laughed at the urban legends about people whose hair had fallen out or who had become permanently impotent. In my arrogance, I would never have dreamed that I would find myself standing outside the Research wing of Guy's Hospital in South East London, five minutes before my screening appointment, at the same time praying that I had found a solution to my financial problems but also wanting to run away as fast as my legs would carry me. I closed my eyes and thought of senoritas and sea trout.

The waiting room was like a headmaster's office – full of nervous guilty boys, guilty of being poor in an expensive city. At first we just sat there looking miserable, fidgeting and trying not to catch anyone's eye, in case they saw the fear. Then a remarkable thing happened. Someone asked for the time with an accent that was more Bloemfontein than Bloomsbury and someone answered with a definite Cape Town "Ja bru, no problem." It was soon apparent that, except for a Kiwi and a dodgy-looking Pom, the rest of us were South Africans. This was much better; I wasn't the only failure. The mood picked up straight away. We were brothers in arms, in desperation, in the beautiful knowledge that we could make the equivalent of a month's salary in four days. Impotence be damned!

The mood changed immediately. We were on a school outing, excited kids on the way to Money World. It was great, we passed lewd comments about the nurses, in Afrikaans of course, and the Kiwi got teased for the choking tendencies of his rugby side. Nobody spoke to the Pom – he was a slightly intimidating, dreadlocked fellow who looked like he seldom felt the need to visit a laundromat.

Then the doctors were ready for us. We filed one by one into curtained-off areas for the beginning of our ordeal. We were poked, prodded, and robbed of our blood. We peed in jars and got wired up to weird bleeping machines that looked perfectly capable of electrocuting us to death. Worst of all, we were questioned intimately by a woman. Shock and horror! Blushing like a 13-year-old girl, I admitted sheepishly that I had never used intravenous drugs, been allergic to penicillin, had heart complaints, or fantasised about Winnie Mandela in a wetsuit. I had not had penetrative sex with a man, had a blood transfusion or had my mental health brought into question (okay, I am willing to lie for a bit of cash).

It eventually came to an end and we gathered for the debrief session. We were told by a stern doctor that from the 20 of us, eight would be chosen who met the criteria of having blood which was free of virus, nicotine and any trace of illegal substances. Looking around at the motley gathering, I got the feeling that they might have to relax the criteria. Those chosen would be paid £150 per day, for each of the five days spent at the centre, and the amount would not be taxed.

I went back to my crappy office job, back to the crappy computer printouts that spewed endlessly from the crappy printer like accountant-themed toilet paper. I waited, not with dread, but with excitement now. And then she called. At the end of the day, I told my supervisor that Friday would be my last day. He didn't seem particularly surprised; I had lasted longer than any temp they'd had. I would have gone out and got drunk, but that £750 glowed at the end of the rainbow of abstinence, more persuasive than 10 nagging mothers.

Monday morning arrived and I met the rest of the pure ones. I was rather surprised to see the mean-looking Pom and didn't feel so special anymore, although he could have been chosen because of his previous drug-testing experience. There were 10 of us; we would all be re-tested for impurities and the two extras were reserves, in case anyone had not been able to make it through the weekend. I was a little nervous, but felt better when I heard one of the other guys talking about his huge Friday night and the copious amounts of Bolivian marching powder that some girl had 'forced' him to take.

And then there were eight. Myself, the Kiwi, the Pom, and then Gerhard from Pretoria, Guy from Cape Town, Pierre from East London, another Dave from Durban and two youngsters from Sandton, would you believe it. One was called Nic and one was called Dimitri, but I never knew which was which before the drugs. They were both 19, in London for six months courtesy of their fathers, and had run out of money after three, hence their presence and no doubt the reason their blood met the criteria. Enough said.

The stern doctor explained that we would receive the dose the next day, at 8am. It was a drug that was being developed to treat children with attention deficit hyperactivity disorder and that two groups, one of them prisoner volunteers, had already been tested on lower doses. We would be connected to a drip throughout the day and would have blood samples taken every 30 minutes until 4pm, and then every two hours after that. We were forbidden to eat anything during the day, and any urine passing would have to be done into large containers labelled with our names and handed to one of the nurses. He assured us that no one had died while doing trials and that the only side effects that they had encountered so far were dizziness and slight headaches. No mention of hair loss or impotence, but they wouldn't, would they?

The complex was like a posh hotel compared with the cramped South London flat that I had been sharing with five other smelly backpackers. We slept in the ward, but it was big and clean and there was a team of friendly young nurses to look after us. There was also a TV room with about a hundred videos, a library, and a dining room. We got three meals a day, but were not allowed anything else and were definitely not allowed out of the building.

There was one other group of guinea pigs in the complex, long-term residents who were testing some sort of psychiatric drug. They looked bizarre, with loads of coloured electrodes permanently connected to their scalps, making them look like new-age Rastafarians. I got a fright when I went into the bathroom that evening to find one of them sobbing over the basin. I left the poor guy alone but noticed him an hour later having a loud, merrily animated conversation in the TV room. It turned out that chronic mood swings were an obvious side-effect of their drug.

Everyone on our ward was in good spirits, although a bit nervous. My bed was next to the Pom, who despite appearances turned out to be a gentle and very friendly fellow. His name was Darra and he was half Greek, and until recently, seemed to have been a professional anti-apartheid protester. As far as the government was concerned, he was two people, both of whom were conveniently on the dole. He had a council flat, but he rented it out and lived in a squat. He did drug trials every now and again, mainly to get money to get to India, where he lived on the beach in Goa for months on end, returning to London with large amounts of Class B drugs sewn into the lining of his luggage, which sorted out his living expenses until he could get on the next drug trial. He was 34 years old but didn't look a day over 40. Everyone else gave him a wide birth, which is a pity because he knew more about South Africa than I did – from his activist days or from sharing drug-trial wards with South Africans, I couldn't say.

We were awoken at 6:30 the next morning and the nurses didn't seem quite as friendly as they had the day before. With cold efficiency, they collected all the pee bottles and went around attaching catheters to everyone's arms. This is where we started to earn our money. Catheters, if you haven't watched ER enough, are little tube things that stick permanently into your arm and allow nurses to draw blood at any time, without turning you into a pincushion. They bloody hurt, though.

At 8am, the first person got their dose, two little white pills and a cup of water to wash it down with. I was second-last in line and had plenty of time to make sure that the first guy didn't fall out of bed or stop breathing or something. They staggered the dose so that the nurses had time to connect people to more bleeping machines while others took blood and so on. The military precision of the whole operation was actually quite comforting, though I kept on expecting a nurse to sigh heavily and pull a sheet over one of my newly deceased colleagues. I guess I'd been watching too much ER.

We had to stay in bed all day, eight hours in total, and it got a bit boring. Every half hour or so, a doctor would come around with a clipboard asking me to describe exactly how I felt. "Well, since Frisbee the gerbil died when I was five, I've had trouble making friends..."

I analysed every little twinge in my body, every pseudo headache, just to tell them something. I wanted to be the best guinea pig ever and earn my money. But there was nothing, actually I felt fantastic – something to do with sleeping in a proper bed and having three square meals a day, I'm sure. I was bit jealous of Pierre's dizzy spells and Guy's headache, and those black spots that Darra was seeing would really have been cool, but by the end of the day, I had absolutely nothing to report except an exceptional urge to go to the toilet.

Later on, they told us that only six of us got the real drug. The other two were given placebos – little white sweets or something. They wouldn't tell us who, but five people got symptoms and three didn't, so there is a good chance that I got the sweet –a bit disappointing, really. We stayed the next three days just to be sure and the blood letting continued, though less frequently. I got pretty good at pool, learned a lot about Goa, and got feverishly excited reading South America On A Shoestring. I also noticed that I wasn't impotent, which was a relief, so to speak.

I said my goodbyes and got a big bear hug from Darra. Blinking against the watery autumn sunshine, I slung my bag over my shoulder and crossed the Thames to London Bridge Station. The cheque seemed to throb warmly in my back pocket and made London feel friendly again. After the peace of the hospital, it hummed in my ears like some great beast of opportunity. The excitement started to well up again. Let the good times roll!

Postscript:

I kept in touch with Darra and met up with him a few months later when we were both back from our travels. I had found a pretty good job at last, so didn't have to take him up on his offer of staying at his squat. He had a brilliant time in India and was negotiating to buy his council flat at half its market value, which he was planning to sell immediately and go overland from Cairo to Cape Town. I said that if he ever found himself in Durban, I knew a few people who could definitely sort him out with a little freelance drug testing.

5 OUR MAN IN BUENOS AIRES

As culture shocks go, arriving from the middle of a UK winter into the Buenos Aires morning rush hour must be about as shocking as it gets. My guidebook said that the city is 'sexy and alive, combining faded European grandeur with Latin passion'. My first impression was that it was very hot and very confusing.

I might have tied about 500 trout flies to prepare for the trip, but with my typical lack of foresight and 'I'll be okay' attitude, I hadn't thought of taking any Spanish lessons. Even a phrasebook would have helped me navigate the bewildering public transport system from the airport into the city centre, where most of the backpacker hostels were. I caught a bus to the train station, then a train ride in the wrong direction and another back again, and finally a very expensive taxi ride.

Three hours and a litre of sweat later, I was dropped outside the hostel that had the best review in my travel guide. Naturally, I hadn't booked ahead, and of course it was full.

Another hour of trudging around in 30-degree heat and I was feeling anything but 'sexy and alive' when I finally checked into a nice little hostel a couple of streets away. I was shown to my room by the beautiful receptionist who didn't speak a word of English, but still babbled away in Spanish without me understanding one single word. I think proper authors would call that 'foreshadowing'.

The room was rather small, but cool and nicely decorated with a window overlooking a courtyard where I could see a few backpacker types relaxing in the sun. There were two sets of bunk beds and while I unpacked, my two new roommates arrived back from their day's sight-seeing. They were athletically attractive Dutch ladies in their early 30s, who both greeted me with a kiss on each cheek. I think they were a couple, but it can be hard to tell with such demonstrative Europeans. They said that they had been cycling their way down from Brazil for the past three months and were full of amazing stories of the sights they had seen and the experiences they had enjoyed.

Despite my exhaustion, I was fizzing with excitement. I thought I would start slowly with a walk around the neighbourhood to get my bearings and then grab one of the steaks that my guidebook went on about so much. I popped into a mini supermarket to get some water and a snack to tide me over, but when I looked at the price tags I thought I was hallucinating with fatigue. A bottle of water and a bag of nuts cost half my daily budget!

I walked out without buying anything and started looking at restaurant menus and the price tags in shop windows. I had a mini panic attack. Everything was unbelievably expensive, like Piccadilly-Circus-tourist-trap expensive. Feeling very deflated, I finally bought some plain noodles from a Chinese supermarket, went back to the hostel to eat them on my own, and then went to bed at 8pm feeling very dejected.

The next morning, I was woken by a strange noise and an alluring smell. The noise was a sort of gentle slurping sound that you might associate with walking barefoot through mud, but that was at odds with the pleasing floral aroma. I opened one quizzical eye and was met with a rather unexpected sight. One of the ladies was standing in the small gap between the beds liberally applying some sort of lotion all over her very tanned and very naked body. She was completely nonplussed when she saw my surprised face, greeting me with a cheery "Good morning!" and continuing her routine.

When I was sure that my blushing cheeks had returned to their normal colour and other parts had realised it was a false alarm and stood down, I joined my new friends for breakfast, intent on picking their brains about how to get by on as little money as possible. To my relief, they said that they'd found Argentina the most expensive country they had passed through, and Buenos Aires was by far the most expensive city. They were struggling not to exceed their US$50 a day each, which was more than double what I had planned to spend.

They explained why our guidebooks were so out of date on how much things cost. Since 1991, the Argentinian Peso had been pegged to the US Dollar in an attempt to prevent the hyperinflation that had affected other South American economies. This had worked to an extent, but with the Argentinian economy now stagnating, a tipping point had been reached and the cost of living had suddenly been pushed through the roof as the country slipped into recession. I had just picked the wrong time to visit.

It became clear that my plans would have to be changed or my four-month trip would grind to a financial halt after six weeks. Even though I would be missing some of the best fishing on the continent, I just couldn't afford to stay in the country. After breakfast, I went straight to a travel agent and booked a series of bus tickets south that would get me the 3,000 kilometres to the border with Chile in about three days.

But first, I gave myself two days to soak up every sight, sound and experience that the glorious city of Buenos Aires could provide – the free ones at least. I walked miles, I admired beautiful old buildings and sumptuous public parks. I almost died trying to cross the famous Avenida 9 de Julio which is 140m wide and has 12 lanes of traffic, traffic that didn't have the same respect for zebra crossings as I was used to. This was a city that did everything on a grand scale, from steaks to boulevards.

On the advice of the guidebook, I visited a bizarre cemetery that had mausoleums bigger than most London houses. As I looked around, I heard a strange wailing noise and came across two old ladies clutching each other and crying theatrically in front of the flower festooned tomb of someone called Eva Perón.

I also spent a lot of time gazing longingly at the multitude of brown-eyed beauties that were everywhere you looked in the city. I had never seen so many pretty girls in my life. Unfortunately, I couldn't speak to them and anyway, most were on the bulging arm of some Latino Adonis. I optimistically bought a Learn Spanish In A Month book.

On the night before I was due to head south, I dressed up in the least crumpled clothes I could find in my bag and joined some other pale backpackers from the hostel for a night on the town. To save money, we bought a few beers in the local supermarket and drank them in the courtyard before heading out into the sultry night, full of expectation as to what hedonistic pleasures the city had in store for us.

The first problem was that nothing seemed to be open. It was a Friday night around 10pm. In the UK, the pubs would be closing in an hour, but here there was hardly a soul on the streets. Peering through the darkened windows of what was obviously a trendy bar, all we could see was an old woman wiping down the tables.

We eventually found a pavement café that served drinks, so sat chatting, nursing our overpriced beers, and watching very little of the world pass by. Nearing midnight when I was just starting to yawn, it definitely felt like there were more people about. A while later, two painfully elegant young couples with movie-star looks breezed past, and as if by magic, the doors of the night club next door opened and they were welcomed inside by a very large doorman. I was quite surprised that the bouncer kissed both girls on the cheek, and then very surprised when he kissed both the men in the same way. Very odd I thought, but maybe they were family or good friends. But the next group got the same treatment, and the next. That was the first of many signs that my South African concept of masculinity didn't really apply on this continent.

We didn't try to get into that club. I'm not sure that my German companions' socks and sandals would have been acceptable anyway. We went walkabout and by 2am Buenos Aires was in full swing. People filled the streets, both young and old. And by young, I mean actual small children out with their parents for an evening stroll. Everywhere we looked were rammed bars and nightclubs where earlier, there had only been dark windows or grey shutters. People that maybe couldn't afford the bars were partying in the streets. The most beautiful crowd that I had ever seen in one place; laughing, dancing, having more fun than I had ever had in my life. And this was in a recession!

I felt shabby, pale, and very very out of my depth, but I loved it. I was philosophical; I had four months in South America – plenty of time for fun and excitement and finding my Latina princess. I called it a night, leaving my Euro companions awkwardly shuffling about on the dancefloor of a small club while all around them couples shimmied their hips with abandon and spun each other around with professional-level skill.

I woke up the next morning with a surprisingly strident hangover, considering how little I had drunk. It was probably from the sensory overload of the Buenos Aires nightlife. No slurping noises this time, but I soon became aware of a rustling sound in the room which suggested that at least one of my roommates was up. Just to be safe, I fired a warning shot by yawning and stretching loudly, before opening my eyes to the rear view of one of the ladies bending over her backpack. Nothing wrong with that, except all she was wearing was a towel, and that was wrapped around her head!

It was time to leave town, but not before a very cold shower.

6 FEAR AND PISCO IN PATAGONIA

The average Chilean man wouldn't be seen dead drinking wine. Even if he did, it would be out of a two-litre box and would be called Gato Negro. He would drink it from a mug in one go, and then challenge you to a hairy-chest competition. Chileans drink Pisco, and they take it very seriously. Pisco is also made from grapes, but that is where the similarities end.

I was now an expert, and had the headache to prove it.

What do you know about Chile? I'm guessing you've tried a nice Chilean red or two, and that is probably where your interest begins and ends. Geographically, it is an odd country. Long and skinny, it stretches for 6,000 kilometres up the west coast of South America. In the North: the driest desert on Earth. In the South: glaciers, rainforest and the wild bleakness of Patagonia. In between: countless sun-kissed beaches and a thousand picture-postcard lakes. I started at the bottom and the plan was to see it all, and do a lot of fishing on the way.

I am sure that up north, closer to the capital Santiago, there are hordes of wine lovers. I am sure that the sunny pavement cafés are full of elegant men, sipping Merlots and discussing opera. I just hadn't met them yet. From what I had seen so far, Chile was a country where men were men and women fetch the drinks.

Chile has a difficult past. Under General Pinochet's dictatorship in the 70s and 80s, thousands of opposition supporters had late-night visits from the secret police and were never heard from again. Thousands more made themselves scarce. Those who could afford it left the country. Those who couldn't went south into the mountains or north into the desert. Fortunately, those times are in the past, but the legacy remains. You won't find a Pinochet Appreciation Society down there.

I was in Punta Arenas, the last town on mainland South America. I wouldn't choose to live there. It was just before Christmas, midsummer, and there was still snow on the hills. The wind blew almost constantly and cut straight through my budget hiking jacket that I had bought in a London charity shop. I wouldn't visit in July. It is far enough south that penguin watching maintains the local tourist trade, and planes from the local airport fly down to Antarctica to drop supplies at the research bases. My plan was to acclimatise for a couple of days after my mammoth bus journey through Argentina, before heading north into Patagonia, one of the best trout-fishing regions in the world.

But my plan changed that first night when I was relaxing in the hostel. It was about 9pm and the sunlight was still shafting through the lounge window, where I sat tying some trout flies.

"What are you doing there, friend?" said a laid-back voice.

It belonged to an American called Bill, who knew perfectly well what I was doing. We got chatting. He said he was also a keen fisherman and had heard that one of the managers at the hostel moonlighted as a fishing guide and might take us gratis, if we arranged the car hire and provided 'refreshments'. I'd heard about the local guides: wise, proud men with deep roots in Patagonia and a deep love for their rugged land. Their services would normally be beyond my budget, so it sounded like a very good deal. Máximo, it turned out, was cut from a different mould. A great bearded bear of a man, he agreed to our deal but insisted that we nip out right then for the first of the 'refreshments'.

Punta Arenas is an old port town and fits the cliché. A derelict seafront with the wooden skeletons of old fishing boats littering the shore, damp and deserted warehouses and most tellingly, a disproportionate collection of bars filled with weathered people getting as wrecked as the boats. Máximo ordered the first round and I paid for it. The barman slapped down three glasses and slopped in a mixture of spirits from label-less bottles.

Máximo said something to the people around us and all of a sudden, we were the centre of attention. We downed our drinks amidst cheers and backslaps from those around. I was a little confused until Máximo explained that we were drinking Pisco, the unofficial national spirit, and he had announced to the bar that we were trying it for the first time.

Everyone wanted to be near us, or near my wallet, perhaps. I soon felt slender fingers on my waist and turned to look into a great pair of brown eyes, beautiful in spite of heavy blue eyeshadow. She had a similarly painted friend who was similarly entwined with Bill, to his obvious discomfort. A table was cleared and we sat down: the five of us, and a squinty-eyed old man who spoke pretty good English. He was an ex-sailor who now seemed to make his living from chaperoning beautiful young women with too much eyeshadow.

He told us the story of Pisco. It originated in Peru and is named for the port that it was first exported from, or the other way around, depending on what version of history you believe. Chile now produces a sweeter version, which the Peruvians claim is not true Pisco, and therefore unworthy of the name. This has resulted in a bitter trade war, with the dispute fought out in the international courts. It is a type of brandy distilled from the Moscatel grape and can be drunk neat, as Old Squinty repeatedly demonstrated, or mixed with lemon juice and egg white to make a Pisco Sour. The ladies mixed it with Coke – a Piscola. I would never admit it in a sailors' bar, but I preferred it that way best.

I felt it in my feet first, a delightful warmth that crept up my body, relaxing my limbs until I was great beanbag of floppy contentment. I should have seen the signs; I should have realised the locals are probably weaned on the stuff. But it was too late. I had met the best group of people ever. I loved them all deeply, and I had to buy drinks to show my love.

With each new round, a toast and another new friend. I was soon stumbling around the bar having animated conversations with large, bearded men, which is difficult as I had only learnt about 30 Spanish words so far, 31 including Pisco. I grouped it with some other words I knew:

"Amigo! Cuatro Piscos mas, por favor!"

Punta Arenas had a new patron that night.

But that was the first night, and I was wiser the next day. The hire car arrived and Bill went off to look for Máximo, who had made an early exit at midnight with one of the eyeshadow twins, "to walk her home", I think he said. I felt a nagging guilt. I was in fishing's Promised Land and I felt rougher than a goat's kneecap.

It took two hours, but we finally hit the road. Any cobwebs were soon blown away as Máximo the alcoholic became Máximo the rally driver. Not wanting to offend my guide, I kept quiet and prayed. Even at 120km/h on dirt roads, it took us an hour to get to the river. We left the main road and followed it upstream on a labyrinth of rutted paths and dirt tracks, occasionally passing signs loudly stating the Spanish equivalent of 'Private Property – Keep Out!'

Máximo did not seem to appreciate the concept of private property. We settled into a system. He approached a closed gate at high speed and slammed on the brakes at the last minute. He then hunched his shoulders and grunted, the signal for me to jump out and open the gate. I had about two seconds to close it again and get back in before he accelerated off in a hail of gravel. Bill didn't appreciate the system. He lay on the back seat moaning gently and turning different shades of green.

We eventually pulled up at the river. It looked beautiful, but I was a little dubious. From my experience, rivers that look perfect usually have you pulling your hair out and converting to spear fishing before lunch. In the clean water, any fish that you see before they see you might as well be vegetarian, for all the interest they show in your fly.

We tackled up and Máximo grunted dismissively at the diminutive contents of my fly box. He extracted a couple of large green Woolly Buggers from his own box and handed them to me, a fly that truly looks like it sounds. Bill decided to head downstream and tottered off, a little unsteady on his legs. Máximo retrieved a tobacco pouch from somewhere personal and promised to join me in a few minutes. I left him under a tree looking very relaxed as the slight wind carried the sweet and distantly familiar smell of his pipe to my nostrils.

We really were in the middle of nowhere – no people, not even cows and only the bustle of the river to be heard. It felt good. I set off upstream with a bounce in my step and a whistle on my lips. It could have been the Pisco, or Máximo's second-hand smoke, or just my joy at having survived the car journey. It certainly had something to do with going fishing for the first time in a country that has always held a mystical attraction for me. Somehow, the sunlight felt warmer, the grass softer, and the bugs friendlier. I felt like Adam, the first fisherman, alone in a wild garden.

I was disturbed from my daydreams by a shadow blocking the sun for an instant. Startled, I looked up, half expecting a pterodactyl to be bearing down on me. It was my first condor, riding the airflow on the ridge above me, closely followed by my second condor and then my third. I had read about these birds, but you have to see one. They are immense, with wingspans up to 12 feet. Cousins of the African vulture, they are scavengers for the most part and lack the grasping talons of the smaller birds of prey. I am sure there are many small Chilean children who are very happy about this.

I gazed in awe at the feat of divine engineering that allowed these giants to soar as if gravity only applied to us human folk. Seeing condors close up would normally make my year, but on that day an ostrich would have to flap over my head to stand out from all the wonder.

Condors aside, it is outsized trout that I am most interested in. I continued upriver, looking for a likely spot. The basic idea of fly fishing is to fool a trout into thinking that a bit of fur and feathers tied to a hook is one of its favourite insect meals. This is often not easy, as trout can be extremely selective and near impossible to catch. To be honest, I was not feeling massively confident with the ungodly green Christmas decoration tied to the end of my line. However, I was too scared to change it, in case Máximo appeared.

I came to a long deep pool and saw the first splash straight away. I had to rub my eyes to make sure it wasn't a dream. I could see trout moving all over the pool. They were feeding on little grey midges that were hatching in the slack water. It has always amazed me that trout as long as your arm will feed on the tiniest of insects, little creatures that could sit for a family portrait on the nail of your finger.

The fish were going mad, rushing around the pool stuffing themselves with the little beasties. Some of them were throwing themselves clear of the water. Big and golden flanked, they flashed their colours at the sun, before crashing back into the water like mini marlin.

Matching the hatch with my size-six Woolly Bugger, I cast across the pool and let the fly sink into the green depths. There was a flash and a yank on my rod and then a horrible slackness – the line had broken. I tied on a heavier cast with trembling hands and attached the second Woolly Bugger. I cast out again and almost immediately, there was another yank. Nothing broke this time. It was the start of a very busy couple of hours.

I don't know how many fish I caught. Lots, and one of them was my biggest ever. I had to follow him a hundred metres downstream and my wrist was aching by the time I got him to hand. I removed the hook from his impressive kype and gently released him to fight another day, a little wiser of Woolly Buggers and South African trout bums.

Returning wearily to the car when the sun dipped below the edge of the valley, I found Bill snoring gently in the backseat. I roused him and was surprised to hear that he had caught nothing and was a bit disappointed with his first taste of Chilean fishing. With uncharacteristic tact, I mumbled something about only hooking a couple myself and went to wake Máximo, who was still prone under his tree. He seemed to have made an attempt at camouflaging himself by covering his face with dried spittle and bits of foliage. He stumbled to the backseat of the car and fell straight back to sleep.

Bill and I were left to find our way out of the labyrinth of tracks, which seemed to protect the valley like some fairy-tale land. But it was no fairy-tale, it was Chile, and I was starting to like it. I was even looking forward to a celebratory Pisco.

7 FROZEN TOES IN THE LAND OF FIRE

It was cold and the wind blasting off the Patagonian ice cap was driving the sleet almost horizontal to the ground. Every now and again, a gust would catch my pack at an angle and send me stumbling off the path. I looked at my watch; I had four hours left to walk the 22km to the entrance of the national park, where I could catch a bus back to the main road where I would hopefully get another bus back to town.

With a bit of luck, I would manage a few hours sleep before getting to the ferry station, where I was due to meet an American I hardly knew, and a guide who was working for free. I was tired, my knees were killing me and I hadn't showered for days, but I just couldn't stop thinking that the next day I would be crossing the Straits of Magellan to Tierra del Fuego and I was going fishing! If my lips weren't numb, I would have been whistling.

Tierra del Fuego, the Land of Fire, is the island off the southern tip of South America shared by Chile and Argentina. Although it existed on maps as early as 1428, it was only named in 1520 by Ferdinand Magellan, the man who history credits with its 'discovery'. The rather romantic name was born when he spotted plumes of smoke rising from the hills as his ship approached land. These turned out to be the signal fires of the indigenous people, whom history has conveniently forgot about.

Structurally, the island is a continuation of the mainland. Its western side is fortified by the coccyx of the Andes, rugged and glaciated, while towards the east it is flat and treeless, like the steppes of eastern Patagonia. From these barren plains drain some of the greatest trout rivers in the world.

The fabled Rio Grande originates in the Chilean west and empties into the Atlantic on the Argentine side. Trout are not native to South America and it is an interesting story how they came to live here. In the 1930s, an Anglo-Argentine engineer called John Goodall was stationed in the tiny town of Rio Grande. Probably getting bored in the little outpost on the edge of the earth, he wondered whether the great clear river that flowed past the town would be a suitable home for the brown trout that he had known in his homeland. He duly imported the fry and released them.

The fingerlings thrived and Mr Goodall must have considered his experiment a great success. The true extent of this success only became apparent some years later, when huge silver-flanked fish mysteriously started appearing in the river. It seems that some of the original fingerlings had wished to continue their travels and had found their way to the salt. This fertile new environment grew them fat and strong, and their instincts brought them back to the Rio Grande to spawn, something their progeny have been doing ever since.

The exceptional sea trout fishery has been carefully managed and results in some spectacular catches. Sea trout average eight to 10 pounds and specimens of up to 35 pounds have been landed. The best fishing is to be had on the estancias close to the sea. These beats are strictly controlled by a handful of lodges, catering to clients who require wallets as fat as the trout they seek. The sea trout fishing on the Chilean side is far less dependable, although the headwaters carry a healthy population of resident fish, and at the right time of year there is always the chance of a trutta grande.

Truth was, I had never planned on visiting Tierra del Fuego. I had heard about the stranglehold that the lodges have on the fishing rights on the Argentinean side, and I wasn't even aware that the headwaters in Chile offered good fishing. Anyway, stark landscapes and howling winds are usually enough to put me off, even if there are monster sea trout to be had.

If there's one thing I've learned on my travels, it's that plans can always be changed and one must never look a gift horse in the mouth. My gift horse was the opportunity to camp and fish with Bill and Máximo. The three of us had made a couple more day trips from Punta Arenas and had some fantastic fishing, but Máximo kept saying that we would have to head into the true wilderness for the best of it. The big man had taken a shine to Bill and had agreed to take him on a 10-day trip for a token fee. I had the feeling that Bill wanted me along to ensure that he didn't demand payment in other ways. I wound him up by humming the duelling banjos tune from Deliverance every now and again.

I agreed to meet up with them a week later, after I had spent Christmas hiking in Torres del Paine National Park with some English friends. Unfortunately, we had been caught in a snowstorm and had to hole up in our tent for a couple of days. I left my friends as soon as the worst of it was over and plotted a direct route to the park's entrance. It was a lot further than I'd calculated; jogging and power walking with a heavy pack full of damp gear, I started to get the twinges in my knees that would haunt me for the next few months.

I just made the bus to Punta Arenas. The hostel had hot water for a change, and I had time to cook myself a huge plate of spaghetti and tie a few more flies before going to bed, where 20lb sea trout swam all night in the rivers of my dreams. Early next morning saw three figures huddled on the bridge of the ferry, squinting into the morning haze as seagulls screeched overhead, penguins bobbed on the glassy sea and the rugged silhouette of Tierra del Fuego loomed from the murk.

With my rudimentary grasp of Spanish, I wasn't sure how my Chilean companion managed to persuade a local in a battered Volvo to drive us the 240 km into the heart of the island, for little more than the cost of breakfast. At first, we followed the curve of a huge bay on a rough gravel road. The wind had started to blow and it became obvious why the only vegetation was low scrub and grass fed on by isolated clumps of unhappy looking cows. Occasionally, we passed the front gates of estancias, elegantly signposted with proud Spanish names and the obligatory cattle skull. Behind, dirt driveways wound into the distance with no sign of human habitation. After an hour of driving and a puncture, we cut away from the coast. On the map, the road we followed was just a thread of red that meandered south before being choked out by contour lines and rivers – a genuine 'road to nowhere'.

As we left the sea behind, the landscape changed. The undulations of the coast became hills, and in the distance, craggy snow-capped peaks. The few trees were contorted and bent away from the west, with 10 shattered trunks on the ground for every one that maintained a precarious hold in the soil. In every valley ran a stream, very trouty, but very exposed and I pictured their speckled residents growing fat and numerous under the tangled banks.

We stopped at a slightly larger stream, the Rio Rusfin – an unusual name and a most unusual piece of water. It wound extravagantly through a shallow valley like a snake, its watery coils threatening to touch on every bend and creating innumerable lies in the little runs and deep holes amongst the clumps of grass. Máximo showed us a spot where a client had caught an eight-pound brown the year before. It was at the outlet of a pool where the stream narrowed so that a man could straddle it. The vegetation formed a tunnel, making a conventional cast impossible – Máximo explained how the client had drifted a rubber lure from the top of the run. I was itching to have a few casts, but we were headed for the Rio Grande and that was still another hour and another puncture away.

The river was big and grey and flushed with snowmelt. It moved like a military parade of stern-faced soldiers, a good cast wide with a strong and a constant flow. Any trout with designs on self-preservation would be attached firmly to the stones, protected by that surging grey army and the gusting wind. My heart sank a little. We hiked downstream and eventually found a barrier of trees that offered some protection from the elements.

By the time we had made camp and tackled up it was past 6pm, which wasn't a problem as there were still five hours of light left. I started fishing a heavily weighted nymph upstream, and then down and across when the wind shifted. I soon realised why Máximo had laughed when I assembled my five-weight. What I was doing probably looked more like kite flying than casting. He had a hefty #8, which I could see him wielding with power and ease a hundred metres upstream. He had caught two small fish and briefly hooked something substantial by the time we took a tea and thaw-out break at 8pm.

I took the opportunity to look through his fly box and noted that just about every fly in there was about two inches long and black. I changed flies to the largest I could find in my collection and set off downstream, looking for a pool or some feature that might break the relentless surge of the river and perhaps be home to my dream fish.

I have always been drawn to remote fishing spots, places where you get the feeling that you are the only person on Earth. In Natal, it is difficult to get away from power lines and roads and the distant roar of a tractor. Even in the Eastern Cape, there are fences and cows to remind you that civilisation is just over the hill. But in that valley, I got the Adam feeling again, like it was just me in this windswept wilderness.

Walking through a crop of trees, I disturbed a family of guanacos, cousins of the llama, which loped off snorting their disapproval at being disturbed. Everywhere along the river were gnawed trees and fishy droppings, evidence of the beavers which were introduced to Tierra del Fuego to attract trappers and traders into the wild interior. When demand for pelts dropped, these hardy people moved on, leaving the population to prosper with no threat from man or beast. I caught sight of them occasionally and if it weren't for their dams, I would have had a tough time crossing the larger tributaries.

Wading through a bog, I almost stood on a family of ducks and watched as one parent hurried the ducklings away while the other distracted my attention with an Oscar-winning rendition of an injured bird in its death throes. With its family safely out of sight, it made a miraculous recovery and flew off to join them.

In a steep-sided valley, I found a section of broken water that ended in a wide pool with overhanging trees and grey-green depths. With the wind at a comfortable angle and my heart beating like a bilge pump, I stripped off line and carefully waded into the flow. I threw my Woolly Bugger across and down and watched the end of the line as it swept into the deep part of the pool. I retrieved when it straightened and was about to start another cast when there was a subtle flash in the depths and my rod jerked in reply.

A little over two pounds, the trout pulled unbelievably hard and made me doubt my ability to handle anything bigger. Without moving an inch, I caught six of its siblings, identical in size and condition and all hooked on the edge of the gravel shelf in front of me. I gave up when the shivering outweighed the fun and started back to camp with a detour to stalk a little fish rising in one of the beaver dams in a side tributary. Máximo and Bill had given up hours ago without catching anything else and were already in their sleeping bags when I got back. We drank whisky and laughed loudly as the wind buffeted our little tent, the light faded to an uneasy grey... and I was glad that I wasn't the only person on Earth after all.

It rained during the night and we awoke to find the Rio Grande swollen and menacing. We decided to head upstream and look for a tributary that Máximo had fished once under similar conditions. As we walked, he told us the story of the time he was guiding a couple of lawyers from the capital Santiago when a local shepherd stopped by their campsite to ask for a cigarette. Máximo gave him a whole box and they had spoken a while. The man said he spent four months at a time in the wilderness tending the landowner's sheep, and had never left the island in his 45 years. He returned the next morning with a lamb, which he slaughtered on the spot and butchered for them, to the obvious shock of the city-slicker clients.

Back at the road, we watched a man and a young boy casting heavy spoons into the churning rapid below the bridge. When we enquired after their luck, the man nodded to the grass behind them, where a great slab of sea trout lay in state. The boy had just caught it; it was as long as his leg and a good deal thicker. He didn't seem particularly excited. We followed the Rio Grande upstream all day across a huge flat plain towards mountains and forests that never seemed to get any closer.

Late in the evening, we made camp in a clump of trees. It was cold and we built a bonfire that got so hot we had to re-pitch the tent further away. A moving lump of fur turned out to be a little fox that circled our fire and then settled down about 30 feet away to watch us. I felt guilty cooking under its hungry gaze, though I shouldn't have worried – the next day I saw it trotting through the grass carrying a large bird and looking very smug.

With only five hours of real darkness, one gets a bit disorientated – there is never any rush to fish and the best time to sleep is when it's raining or too windy. The day was stormy and we sat tight as lightning flashed over the distant mountains and brown clouds swirled around the plain like drunken dancing ghosts. Later, the sky cleared and the wind dropped to nothing. For the first time on Tierra del Fuego I heard silence, interrupted by the occasional scream of a recently widowed hat objected to the presence of our fox.

It was past 10pm when I made for a big bend near the camp. I hoped that the weird climatic conditions would provoke a reaction from the big fish that had largely been keeping to themselves. The river was like oil slipping past in the yellow light, no insects hatched and no fin disturbed the surface. I sat on a log and watched awhile, thoroughly enjoying myself without even wetting my line. I eventually felt obliged to have a few casts and at just after 11pm, a small rainbow ruined a perfectly fishless day by impaling itself on my sunken nymph. An almost full moon shone in the sky and with no wind, it was hardly cold at all. Máximo and Bill joined me and we must have disturbed that little fox's full-belly sleep as we cast our flies by moonlight and our voices carried across the silence of that great plain, until the time when normal fishermen are long since in bed.

Tierra del Fuego is awesome. It is rugged and lonely and one of the most beautiful places I have ever visited. The fishing opportunities are immense and with the right attitude and the right equipment, you can enjoy one of the most unique wilderness-fishing experiences in the world. There are areas in the south with superb rivers that are completely inaccessible, unless you enjoy a good hike or are on horseback. This is apparently the transport of choice, as the local nags are tough as leather, don't get flat tyres, and can always find their way home when you get lost.

There are no roads – let alone accommodation – in the remote areas, so you will be camping and carrying your equipment on your back. Equipment needs to be of the highest quality, it is an extreme place and you don't want to be shivering in your budget sleeping bag when your cheap tent flies away in the night. For the fishing, I would recommend at least a seven-weight rod with a fast action. You will need the extra power to negate the wind and to subdue any big sea trout that you might hook. The water is freezing, even in January, so a good pair of waders is essential.

In retrospect, my biggest liability was my fly box. I got the feeling that for 90 per cent of the time, my lightly weighted flies were sailing three feet over the trouts' heads. Máximo caught the most fish by far using big, heavily weighted streamer patterns. He only started fishing seriously in the late afternoon and would carry on until it was dark.

His biggest fish was a 16-pound monster that he took after sunset on the ugliest black-and-red streamer fly that I have ever seen. I caught plenty of the small resident trout, but the big sea trout eluded me. I didn't care one bit, though.

After a few more days, I had to head back to civilisation and left Máximo and Bill to follow the tributary that we eventually found. I set off at first light with a bottle of water and a chocolate bar to sustain me until I got back to town that afternoon. Máximo pointed me in the direction of the road and assured me that even though there was very little civilian traffic that far south, there were always logging trucks taking product to the port. I reached the road with no problem and, full of energy and optimism, started walking when no trucks had passed and I had started to get a bit cold.

To cut a long and painful story short, no trucks came and I only got back to town at 10pm the following evening after hiking for a day and a half and spending an uncomfortable night in the forest with no tent, water or food. Sleep came between rainstorms and not unreasonable fears of being trampled by a guanaco. I was eventually picked up by a weather-beaten old farmer, with a large bull in the back of his truck. He chattered away in an unfathomable dialect while I nodded knowingly and counted down the mile markers to town, a shower and a hot meal.

Postscript:

I later found out that we had been trespassing the entire week that we fished. Máximo might have had a loose agreement with the local landowners, but I doubt it. I think he simply relied on his innate charm and that the chances of getting caught were extremely slim.

8 NEW FRIENDS AND INNOCENT FISH

I'd been in Coyhaique for a few days fishing the fabled Rio Simpson that flows westwards from the Patagonian Andes, past the town, and then 50km to the sea alongside the main road. This suited me perfectly, as my knees were still aching from the abuse of the previous weeks and it was no problem to hitch downstream, fish until my knees gave up and then thumb a lift back into town a couple of hours before dark. It was a little frustrating missing the evening rise when the wind dropped and the bigger fish started moving to the almost continuous caddis hatch, but at least I was fishing.

Coyhaique is a town of about 40,000 people and is situated on the Camino Austral, the fragmented Chilean southern highway, which means that the only way to get there is by plane, ferry, or the long way round though Argentina. Within a 50km radius of the town is some of the best accessible fishing in the country and as a result, it is a popular base for visiting anglers, most of whom move onto one of the $500-a-day lodges which operate in the region. I had planned to spend a week hiking and fishing up one of the more inaccessible valleys towards the border with Argentina, but my ruined knees would have made that uncomfortable and a bit too dangerous.

The Simpson is a renowned dry fly river where, on warm days, there will be all sorts of insects hatching, sending the fish a bit dilly. I am told that in hopper season it can get ridiculous, with the trout seemingly intent on suicide. I took fish on all sorts of floating flies, even on the weird foam ants with rubber legs that they sold at the local fishing shop. When they got a bit shy to rise, they would eat a small nymph with gusto.

Risking a charge of sacrilege, I even tried one of Máximo's big green Woolly Buggers that had worked so well further south, and took two salmon-like rainbows from a deep, foamy pool that was so close to the road that I had to stop casting when a car drove past. I quickly reverted to more socially acceptable tactics for fear of a tongue lashing from one of the size-18 Elk Winged Caddis brigade, whom I regularly encountered in all their designer river-wear plumage.

The Simpson was good, but it was a little crowded and I hadn't come to Chile to get patronised by catalogue-fishermen and watch dinky kids with coffee-can reels catch bigger fish than me. On the day before I was due to move on, I decided to hitch out of town and then follow a little stream to its source at a lake that was rumoured to grow some respectable fish.

Limping along and covered in dust, I was surprised when a late model 4x4 skidded to a stop and a big blonde head leant out of the window and asked where I was headed with 'that pretty little fly rod, was it a nine-foot five-weight?' And so I made the acquaintance of John and Johnny from Rhode Island, New York. They quickly made room amongst their plethora of rod cases and camping equipment and plied me with biscuits and diet cola as we bumped along in their hire car, following a hand-drawn map which, according to my new best friends, would lead us to flyfishing utopia. Their enthusiasm was infectious and I happily abandoned my previous plan. It had been a couple of weeks since I had spoken English and we were rattling and shaking further and further off the beaten track, happy in the cosy bosom of camaraderie.

The scenery in this part of Chile is breathtaking. Not quite as rugged as further south, but with much better weather. The landscape also creates unusual microclimates, so you can never be sure what sort of vegetation or fishing conditions you are going to get round the next corner. At one stage, Johnny was comparing the surroundings to northern Montana and only 15 minutes later, we were edging our way up a tight valley that reminded John very closely of a Norwegian fjord.

After 40 kilometres and two life stories I came to my senses and started to think about getting home that evening. According to the map, which should have had 'not to scale' written in large letters across the top, we were only halfway to utopia, and it looked like we were going to have to cross an imposing-looking watershed to get there. Feeling like I had just run over their cat, I broke the news that I wouldn't be able to accompany them on their quest and should really get out if I didn't want to spend the night in the forest again. After warm goodbyes and promises to email, I was left on the side of the road, emotionally dishevelled as the John and Johnny road show disappeared in a cloud of dust, like some whirlwind of goodwill.

As they tend to at times like this, my thoughts turned to trout. For the past half hour, we had been in a thickly forested valley. Every now and again, I had caught glimpses of a stream through the trees. It was nameless on my map, but flowed into a lake about three kilometres away that was well known for its trophy-sized fish. I scrambled down the steep slope, pushing through dense foliage and feeling more like Indiana Jones than Gary Borger.

The stream was clear, fast, and icy cold. At first, I thought I had made a horrible mistake and that it didn't hold any trout. I gingerly made my way downstream, straining my eyes to spot a movement in the dappled shadows. It didn't take long as a slender shape at the back of a pool slowly grew fins and then shot off when I got too close. It would have been impossible to make a cast and at least I had confirmed that there were fish in these here waters, as my new friends would have said.

I continued on my way, picking through the thick vegetation and doing a bit of rock climbing as the stream quickly lost altitude. At one stage, I was perched on a ledge above a long pool flanked by vertical cliffs. In the slack water towards the end of the pool I spotted a large trout, probably only about three pounds, but looking very out of place in the rushing little stream. I tried dangling my line down... but the fish understandably ignored the strange grasshopper that managed to hover above the water before settling with a plop.

I soon got frustrated. I had covered more than a kilometre and hadn't been able to find a decent stretch of water where I could get a cast in. Down the valley, I caught glimpses of the lake through the trees. Its surface was a mess of chop and foam as the west wind funnelled down the gorge. Any fishing was going to have to be done on my sheltered little stream. I slowed down and came to a pool whose bottom was silt and fallen leaves rather than pebbles. The banks were heavily wooded, but it looked very fishy and I crept through the trees peering into the depths. I soon spotted a fish holding station near the bank, only a rod length from where I stood behind a tree. As my eyes became accustomed to the shadows I saw another, and then another that was tight against the bank under my feet. I could just see her tail and my heart quickened to see how wide it was.

The fish were all on the bottom, not moving except for an almost indiscernible sway of tail and fin. I still had the hopper on, so I carefully stepped backwards and prepared my rod. I pulled the leader out until just a bit of flyline was past the end eye. I then carefully moved into position, holding the rod on the middle join. I reckoned on getting about three meters of drift if I could drop the fly just where some branches reached into the water. I was confident that I couldn't be seen and it was just the movement of the rod that would have alerted the fish, which I could now see perfectly below me, just four or five feet away.

I got lucky on the first attempt and the fly drifted slowly over a fish of about 30cms. Immediately, I could see its attitude change. The pectoral fins began to move quickly and I am sure that it was looking upward. All of a sudden, a smaller fish that I hadn't seen rose off the bottom and prodded the fly with its nose. It followed it all the way until it skidded across the surface and then disappeared. I realised that I had been holding my breath for the past 20 seconds and exhaled violently. I couldn't remember the last time I got excited about a fish no bigger than my hand.

I tried a couple more drifts, but only succeeded in agitating the bigger fish. I retreated and had a rethink about tactics. I looked through my box and decided on a plump little nymph that was quite heavily weighted. I crept back into position and swung the fly towards the branches. It landed with a plop and sank right towards a fish on the bottom. The fish immediately swung around and had a good look at the fly before it hit the bottom and stuck in the silt. It then lost interest altogether and returned to its station. I tried several more times, with similar results. Once an individual fish had followed a drift, it would not even react to the fly again.

I was completely absorbed in my little game that was very unlike fly fishing and would have looked ridiculous to anyone watching. It was a good thing that I was completely alone. I was determined to hook one of these trusting trout that swam like speckled goldfish at my feet. My saviour came quite by mistake and stopped me just short of sharpening a stick and attempting to impale one.

I had moved a little downstream and changed to an even smaller nymph, which got a bit of attention, but not enough to result in a strike. As before, one or two of the palm-sized trout would follow and then nervously retreat as soon as there was a hint of drag. They were innocent, but their self-preservation instincts were firmly intact. Then on one of the drifts, the fly hit the bottom and stuck. I left it there for a couple of minutes, watching impotently and seriously considering the spear option. When I picked it up, it rose seductively in a little puff of silt and the nearest fish rushed forward and confidently sucked it in. My knee-jerk reaction was to lift my arm, which whipped the fly from the fish's lips and resulted in a tangle of tippet in the branches above my head.

With my new tactic, I managed two more hook-ups, though neither stuck. I just couldn't set the hook properly with only half a rod. I was amazed how often a fish would suck in the fly, spit it out again, only to suck it in again, without the rod tip registering any take. If I hadn't been watching, I would have been none the wiser. It was also interesting that the fly was attractive as long as it was rising from the bottom, and would be completely ignored when it was going the other way.

I eventually tired of my game and carried on towards the lake. The stream joined another tributary and came out into an open valley where I took a nice rainbow from the broken water and nothing from a series of deep emerald-tinged pools that looked like something from a fly-fishing dream. I followed the edge of the lake and was lucky to find some picnickers who offered me chicken drumsticks and a lift back to Coyhaique. The kids climbed all over me in the back seat, enthralled by the flies on my jacket. The parents were more interested in what I was doing wandering around the mountains with a long whippy stick. I spent the journey doing my best to explain, in my broken Spanish, the concept of fly fishing. After the events of the day, I wasn't sure I understood it myself.

9 A FINAL FLING

I loved Chile and stayed there way too long. Apart from the amazing scenery and glorious fishing, I have never met people as friendly, accommodating and generous. Everyone was keen to talk and I got invited into private homes countless times. My rubbish Spanish was a bit of a hindrance, but it didn't seem to matter. I once stayed for two days with a couple of female teachers who didn't speak a word of English but who fed me until I was ready to burst and insisted on taking me on an extended tour of their town and surrounding countryside. When I left, they presented me with a full-size and ornately carved sword, which I carried with me self-consciously for a couple of days before donating it to some kids that followed me down the street in Santiago practising the only English they seemed to know – "Fuck you, Mister!", "Motherfucker!"

I was starting to run out of time and money and still had to make it the 5,000 kilometres overland to Ecuador. I had perhaps fished a bit too much and found myself hankering to see some of the sights that backpackers heading the opposite way on the Gringo trail had enthused about. I was also getting a bit lonely, to be honest. I'd had a brief and mostly platonic romance with a German girl in a hostel down south who was waiting to get on one of the research ships going down to Antarctica. She was very lovely, but in the five days of our acquaintance, I noticed that she didn't change her clothes and hadn't been near the shower room. I may be feral, but I'm definitely a fan of personal hygiene. That relationship fizzled out pretty quickly. I met plenty of local girls and they were very friendly, but with a strict Catholic upbringing, they were very much off limits, as far as I was concerned.

So I hit the backpacker trail with vengeance, bussing up the Pan-American Highway through the desert of Northern Chile, finally reaching the little town of San Pedro de Atacama where it famously only rains every five years. Yet it had rained heavily the day before I arrived and I was surprised to see a river flowing down the main street. Hostel beds were a bit hard to find, as a lot of the mud houses had partially collapsed in the deluge.

I joined a three day tour that would take me over the Andes into Bolivia. Leaving before sunrise, the convoy of 4x4s climbed the astounding Portezuelo del Cajón pass up to the border. In just 45km, the road rises 4,000 metres to a high point of over 6,000 metres above sea level. Bear in mind that Everest Base Camp is at an altitude of 5,300 metres and you will understand why I was feeling a bit light-headed in the thin air.

The border post was just a rickety shack, manned by two unfortunate Bolivian soldiers who didn't seem so happy to be there. With no other buildings visible for miles around, God knows where they slept or even answered the call of nature. By this time, nature was calling me rather urgently, and I was not sure that I could answer. The only suitable shelter I could see was one large rock about the size of a car a hundred yards away from the shack. I surreptitiously sidled over to find hundreds of freeze-dried turds dotted around behind it, like little white monuments to the demise of dignity. I gladly added to the collection and the wind thankfully disposed of my toilet paper in the opposite direction to where the vehicles were parked. Several others from the tour took turns following my lead, and I was very happy I had been the first.

On the first night, we stayed in a ramshackle refugio at the base of a small hill that overlooked a big lagoon populated with hundreds of bright-pink flamingos. In the background loomed the outline of an enormous volcano, and with the steam of the sulphur springs it seemed like a scene from some science-fiction film. I thought I could get an even better photo from the top of the hill, so I optimistically started the short climb. After 20 paces, I was panting and wheezing like an asthmatic geriatric and had to abort to recover on a rock. That night I stared at the ceiling for hours, despite my weariness. Insomnia is another symptom of altitude sickness.

For the next two days, we didn't see another human being, just mountains, volcanoes, and dust. It was like being on the moon. The nights were freezing and the days were boiling hot. A bone-dry wind blew almost continuously and my skin dried and flaked off. On the plus side, the nasty athlete's foot I had been nursing from all the wet wading I had been doing disappeared within two days. The place was inhospitable even to foot fungi.

On the final day, we were due to cross the Salar de Uyuni. I had heard it mentioned by other backpackers, and the guidebook had quite a big section on it that I hadn't had the energy to read. I gathered that it was a big salt flat, which didn't sound terribly exciting, to be honest. I was totally unprepared for the mind-altering experience that it turned out to be, quite possibly the highlight of my whole trip; the non-fishing highlight at least.

It is a 'big salt flat' in the same way that Bill Gates is 'quite well off'. At over 10,000 square kilometres, it is actually the largest salt flat in the world, with the horizon bending away with the curvature of the earth. With no pollutants or sediment, the surface is blindly white and the whole place just doesn't seem like it belongs on planet Earth. What made it truly remarkable was that it had an inch of water on it from the recent rains that had tried to wipe San Pedro off the map. This reflected the pale blue sky and the distant snow-covered peaks, giving them the appearance of giant chunks of rock floating in space. We sat on the roof of the 4x4s clinging on as they belted across the flats for three hours, our minds trying to trick us into believing that we were flying through the clouds. It was trippy.

Bolivia is not an easy country to travel around. It is a geography teacher's dream with more than its fair share of topographical features. But that is the problem; whenever you want to get somewhere, there seems to be a range of mountains, a jungle, or some huge river in the way. Every trip takes a lot longer than you expect and invariably, the bus or boat or truck breaks down, eventually getting fixed by some wiry old guy that appears from nowhere with a pair of pliers and a roll of duct tape. Health and safety is not really a thing.

Stopping for the night in a small mining town, I introduced myself to an Irish couple in the hotel as like me, they were very obviously not local. Eamonn in particular stood out like a sore thumb being a lanky

6' 3", with red hair and freckles. I joined them on a tour of a local silver mine where deep underground, the guide got us to light sticks of dynamite and throw them down a disused shaft. The explosions almost deafened us and we got showered in a hail of dust and rock fragments. I'm not sure who did that risk assessment.

That evening, to celebrate being alive, we went to a small bar that had a karaoke machine well stocked with Western songs, as well as the usual Ricky Martin crowd-pleasers. The only thing worse than my dancing is my singing, but Eamonn got up and said in excellent Spanish "I am a long way from home, and this is a song that reminds me of my country." He then launched into a heart-rending rendition of Danny Boy, which brought a tear to my eye and got a standing ovation from the room full of hardened Bolivian miners.

Moving on, I headed east on the most terrifying bus ride of my life – dropping down from the highlands into the thick jungle of the upper Amazon, on a dirt road that only seemed wide enough for one and a half vehicles. When we came to a bus or truck coming the other way, the two vehicles would have to inch past each other with tyres just about hanging off the edge of the sheer cliff face that dropped thousands of feet down into the valley. The view was breathtaking, but I was too scared to cross to the other side of the bus to take pictures in case I caused it to topple off. Every couple of kilometres, we passed a small cross on the side of the road adorned with plastic flowers and maybe a faded photograph or two. My now very grubby travel guide told me that these were memorials to the victims of previous bus accidents. Bolivia seemed like a very easy country to die in.

The terrain finally levelled off as we dropped down into the jungle, and I felt brave enough to look out the window again. It was hot and humid and with the wet season in full swing, there was water everywhere. We reached a small village on the banks of the Río Ichilo, a major tributary of the Amazon, which it joins thousands of kilometres away in Brazil. Here, we learned the bad news that a major landslide had blocked the only road ahead. There was literally nowhere to stay in the village and if we wanted to leave by road, the only option would be to double-back on Deathwish Highway, which I was in no hurry to do.

Luckily, some other backpackers on the bus were a lot more proactive than me and had negotiated with a barge captain to get a lift downriver to the first town on the other side of the closed road. I happily joined them. The barge was very old and very knackered but with the four-day trip costing us only $25 each, I wasn't expecting luxury. That said, when we were already a few hours downriver, I was a little put out to discover that there was nowhere for us to sleep.

The captain had his own small room and then the cook and deckhand slept in whatever floor space they could find. The hold of the barge was filled with rusty gas canisters that seemed to be slowly leaking their contents, so that wasn't an option. The only free space was on the roof, which wasn't exactly flat. We managed to rig a system of ropes to hang our mosquito nets over and slept under the stars. Unfortunately, the stars were soon obscured by thick clouds and in the middle of the night, it started raining heavily again. That was a miserable night, I can tell you.

The next day, the captain took pity on us and found some wooden planks from somewhere that we balanced on top of the gas canisters in the hold to make serviceable sleeping platforms. At least it was dry, and the smell of leaking butane blocked out the smells that we were producing ourselves after the very unusual meals that the cook came up with.

Despite the hardships, it was a memorable four days, like living in the middle of a nature documentary. We saw pink river dolphins cavorting in the wake of the barge, turtles sunning themselves on logs and lots of alligators malevolently eyeing us up as we motored slowly past. In the evenings, whole clans of capybaras, wild pig and deer would appear on the riverbank to have a drink and hang about. When the barge pulled over for maintenance we swam in the river, except in places where the captain shook his head and made snapping motions with his hands. I joined the deckhand fishing for catfish with pieces of banana as bait and they tasted surprisingly good cooked over hot coals. When we used bits of catfish as bait, we caught piranha, and they tasted even better.

Other than the stops to apply bits of tape to various parts of the engine, the barge kept going from dawn to dusk. With the intense heat, the continuous throb of the diesel engine and the fumes from the gas canisters, I genuinely got an inkling of what it must be like to go insane. It didn't help that one of the other backpackers was a curvaceous Belgian girl who spent her days lounging in a bikini on the roof of the barge, languidly scratching her mosquito bites while her boyfriend smoked incessantly and listened to heavy-metal music on his Walkman.

We finally arrived at the next town, but I genuinely have no memory of it, or catching the bus to the capital, La Paz. Google just told me that one of the side effects of inhaling butane is memory loss, so that might be it. Or maybe I've just repressed the memory of yet another traumatic bus ride.

Crossing into Peru and onwards to the city of Puno, I felt unsafe for the first time on the whole trip. I had been warned that it was a bit of crime hotspot, which isn't unusual in the cities, but walking from the bus station to the hotel it really felt like every pair of eyes was sizing me up for a quick stab-and-dash robbery. My train wasn't due to leave until late the next day, so I holed up in my hotel room for the next 30 hours, trying to read Gabriel García Márquez like a proper backpacker, but mostly watching perplexing Spanish game shows on the small TV. When it was time to go, I got a taxi to pick me up from right outside the hotel.

So onwards into Peru, along the shore of the magnificent Lake Titicaca and forward to the mountain town of Cusco, which is the launching point for the Inca Trail to the lost city of Machu Picchu, and as I quickly discovered, the backpacker party capital of South America. It was like being in Magaluf; you couldn't walk 20 yards without some dreadlocked Scandinavian passing you a flier for a bar, or free entry to a nightclub. Having spent weeks and weeks up in the mountains chasing trout, it all came as a bit of a shock to be surrounded by blonde people my own age, speaking English, and having a great deal of fun.

I had met two other South African guys on the train and gladly hung around town with them for a couple of days. Brad was a big, good-looking chap who was also extremely charming and articulate. His mate was more of a hippy type, skinny with longish blonde hair. But the local ladies absolutely loved him, following us down the streets of Cusco shouting "Bon Jovi, Bon Jovi!". So basically, I didn't get a look in with any of the girls we met. Even if I got chatting to one in the hostel, as soon as Brad arrived, he would muscle in with his big hazel eyes and sparkling repartee. It was starting to grate on me a bit;

the brief fumble with the soap-shy German girl back in Chile seemed a very long time ago.

I had been considering doing the Inca Trail myself, but was worried about my knees, and the cost. It is a tough four-day guided hike through some of the most scenic valleys and passes of the high Andes, culminating in a 4am start to enjoy the "magical spectacle" of watching the sun rise over the ruins of Machu Picchu. Brad wouldn't take no for an answer though, and I agreed that I would join them in doing it solo to save money. We booked the train for 8am the next morning that would take us to the start of the trail, and then decided to celebrate our last night in Cusco by going for a couple of drinks.

One thing led to another and at 6am, we were finally kicked out of a nightclub after one of the best nights of my life. Bon Jovi had disappeared with a local girl at about 2am and Brad was very much the worse for wear, doing an impromptu pole dance on a lamp post and singing "I'm so pretty, oh so pretty!" at the top of his voice, before collapsing giggling in a heap. We have remained good friends and it didn't come as a huge surprise when he leapt out of the closet a couple of years later.

It was left to me to run back to the hostel to get our backpacks which, with uncharacteristic forethought, we had packed the night before. It soon became very apparent that I was not going to be able to carry three large packs all the way back into town on my own. I could carry two and drag one for a few yards and then have to rest. Luckily, two old ladies in traditional Peruvian dress took pity on me, each hoisting a pack onto their backs and setting off for the train station at pace without even asking if that was my destination. When we got there, I tried to give them some money, but they waved me off laughing loudly and probably saying, "This skinny gringo really needs to toughen up!"

I found Brad and we made our way to the platform hoping that Bon Jovi would find the note I had left for him at the hostel. He eventually turned up looking a bit sheepish just before the train departed. He also hadn't slept a wink, though I suspect for very different reasons.

Our carriage was full of other people also doing the Inca trail. A handful were going solo like us, but most were part of organised tours with guides and porters who carried their bags and went ahead to make camp for the evening. Glowing with health and vitality and clad head to toe in North Face, we grew to hate those bastards.

None of us were feeling our best, but Brad was in particular distress. He refused any food and spent the two-hour trip moaning and running off to the toilet every few minutes. We were finally dropped at the trail head and in no time, fell behind the other groups with their porters, normal blood alcohol levels and eight hours' blissful sleep.

Each day of the Inca Trail is about a 15-kilometre hike before you get to a series of basic camping spots excavated out of the rocky ground. After a very hard day and lots of breaks, we finally spotted some bright yellow tents in the distance and managed to drag ourselves the last mile to where the other groups were already sitting around campfires eating cookies and sipping fresh coffee.

The problem, we quickly discovered, was that all the free space was taken. In the steep rocky terrain, there literally wasn't a spare foot for us to pitch our tent. There was nothing else for it, we would have to carry on until we found some flat ground, or the first of the second-night campsites. Brad celebrated this realisation by throwing up voluminously once again. The North Face Bastards waved smugly as we trudged back to the trail.

What followed was possibly the hardest five hours of my life. The path was getting steeper and steeper, and with every step it felt like an unseen assailant was sticking needles in my knee joints. I was feeling dizzy from the altitude and nauseous as I sweated out the last of the tequila. Brad was suffering even more, though. He couldn't keep any liquid down and was probably dangerously dehydrated. At one point, we almost lost him over a precipice when he toppled over.

Bon Jovi, on the other hand, was like some hairy Duracell bunny. He carried on and on, one foot in front of the other, repeating his mantra every few yards: "Slow and steady boys, slow and steady." He even took some gear from Brad and me to lighten our loads, until his pack seemed to dwarf his slight frame. I fell in behind him, watching his knackered leather boots take step after step, mentally dragging me up the mountain.

I really don't know how, but we eventually made it to the next campsite, which – mercifully – was empty. Brad collapsed in a heap, leaving us to put the tent up in the gloom and cook up some dehydrated meatballs and spaghetti, which we were quite possibly the first people ever to enjoy. We then dragged the comatose Brad into the tent and collapsed ourselves, to sleep for 12 hours straight.

I hadn't even noticed the scenery the night before, but leaving the tent the next morning, I realised what an amazing spot it was. We were high up the valley, camped on a ledge about half the size of a tennis court, with sheer cliff faces on three sides. The mist and cloud had cleared and the air was crisp and clear. I could see at least 20 kilometres down the valley and above us, in every direction, were jagged peaks dusted in snow. It was almost worth the pain of getting there, but not quite. I had the most scenic morning pee of my life and finished just in time to avoid exposing myself to the first of the porters who were jogging up the rocky path barefoot, cheerfully chatting and carrying two backpacks each.

The scenery stayed amazing, but the next two days were tough. We never had time to fully recover from that first day and with the altitude sickness, even some of the North Face posse started to struggle. On the final morning, it was all too easy to switch off the 4am alarm when everyone else was waking up for the final two-hour push to see the sunrise at Machu Pichu. We eventually got there just before midday and were very impressed with the place, despite the 300 Japanese tourists that had got the early train and were already swarming all over it.

With only 10 days until my flight left for London I needed to rest. I spent most of my remaining money on a flight from Cusco to the far north of Peru, where it was a simple hop over the border into Ecuador and a week's R&R in the little surfer's village of Montañita. It was like heaven. Ecuador is a far more westernised country than Bolivia and Peru, though just as cheap. There were even some 'normal' holidaymakers in town, escaping from a Northern Hemisphere winter for some sun and surf.

I could afford a surprisingly nice hotel and slept in the same double bed for seven days straight for the first time in six months. I lazed on the beach and swam in the ocean, which was crystal clear and as warm as bath water. Best of all, I befriended two lovely Canadian ladies who were on a two-week holiday from Toronto to learn to surf, and who seemed to have some kind of eating disorder. I joined them at a different restaurant every night where they would order a huge plate of some local delicacy and then only eat a few mouthfuls, leaving me to hoover up the leftovers like some walking waste-disposal unit.

Finally, it was time for a last bus trip to Quito, the mad, bad capital of Ecuador. As the bus trundled along the mercifully unlethal road, I gazed out the window at the endless banana plantations and distant views of smoking volcanoes. Naked kids waved from the side of the road, and guys on mopeds zoomed past carrying everything from a full-sized mattress to an actual live pig.

I thought back to that first day in Buenos Aires when a bit of heat and a confusing train timetable seemed like a culture shock. Now I was shaggy haired, deeply tanned, and as scrawny as a rake. Covered in scabs and scars from a thousand mosquito bites and countless blisters I was certainly no film star, but my Spanish was vastly improved and I had learned to eat like a local and survive on just a few dollars a day. But to be honest, I was totally worn out and couldn't wait to get back to the relative luxuries of London, and to girls that didn't signal their virtue with gold crucifixes around their necks.

Arriving safely in Quito, I found another amazingly cheap hotel and was left with a small wad of Ecuadorian Sucre that I doubted I would be able to exchange for pounds back in London. With no one to buy gifts for, the obvious thing to do was to spend it having a quiet drink in the bar next door to the hotel. With my flight leaving at 10am the next morning, I wanted to be fresh and hangover free, so this was definitely not going to be a repeat of Cusco. The guidebook was also full of dire warnings about how dangerous the streets of Quito could be after dark, so I didn't want to stray too far. I had a beer and a couple of games of pool on the very wonky table, but this was soon pushed to one side to make way for the ubiquitous dancefloor. Ricky Martin was soon Livin' La Vida Loca at top volume, and I had a final opportunity to demonstrate that my sense of rhythm hadn't improved at all.

Around midnight, I was just thinking it was probably time to head to bed when I noticed a girl run into the bar in tears, looking over her shoulder as she pushed her way across the dancefloor. I would like to say I approached her with gallant intentions, but she was very pretty, Brad and Bon Jovi weren't there to interfere and I finally had a bit of confidence in my Spanish. Maybe this was my Latina princess needing a knight in shining armour?

I calmed her down, bought her a Coke with the last of my money and found out her name was Lucia and why she was so upset. Wiping the tears from her eyes, she told me that she had been walking home from work and had seen two policemen beating someone up in an alley down the road. They had seen her and started to give chase, but she was too quick and had given them the slip, escaping into the bar just to be safe. She was terrified of bumping into them again, so I sat with her for a bit and then offered to walk her home. She agreed, but said that I was only walking her home, no funny business, and I definitely wasn't allowed into her house as she boarded with a very strict couple who didn't allow visitors. If they found a gringo in the house, we would both be in big trouble. She stared at me meaningfully with her dark eyes and drew her finger across her throat to emphasise the point.

We left the bar and as we walked through the bustling streets arm in arm pretending to be just another couple (my idea), she told me she was from a provincial town and was studying a Masters in Economics at the university in Quito. She also worked part time in a hotel laundry to pay her way. She couldn't believe that I had been doing nothing but wandering around the continent for the past four months and was going back to London with no job lined up, no family support, and nowhere to stay. She seemed genuinely concerned for my welfare, which was quite ironic given our current situation. "I'll be okay," I said, heroically.

At least she was laughing now. I tried to ask her age – "Cuántos años?" but it turns out that what I actually asked was "How many anuses have you got?"

"Only the one," she giggled, in perfect English.

It was so good to talk to a girl and even better to have my arm around one. We didn't stop pretending to be a couple even after we had left the city centre and I was a bit disappointed when we finally reached the compound where she lived. It was an imposing-looking three-storey building with a high wall topped by razor wire, making it look more like criminal's stronghold than the home of a princess. She unlocked the metal gate and I was about to go in for a final goodbye hug, when a shifty-looking character who had been walking behind us ran up and thrust a very large screwdriver up to my face, shouting at me in Spanish: "Give me money or I will ventilate you!" – although I may not have got that exactly right.

Before I could react, my street-savvy friend pushed the bandido away and dragged me into the compound, slamming the self-locking door in his face.

What to do now? I was stuck between a crazed mugger on the other side of the wall and the possibly violent boarding-house owners asleep upstairs. Lucia took pity on me and said that if I was very, very quiet and left by 6am, I could stay over in her room.

We took off our shoes and tiptoed up to the top floor on shiny polished stairs that squeaked maddeningly with every step. Her room was small and only had a single bed, but she was only little and we managed to fit. This sounded like all my dreams coming true, but with the delayed shock of our encounter with Señor Stabby, I was suddenly feeling sick to the stomach and romance was the last thing on my mind.

Lucia must have realised this, giving me a slightly lingering peck on the lips, and then falling asleep snuggled into my armpit. There was no way I was going to risk shutting my eyes. I was terrified of being caught in bed with Lucia, but mostly I was terrified of falling asleep and missing my flight back to safe and dull old England.

After many hours staring into the darkness and surreptitiously stroking Lucia's hair, a dull grey started to show around the edges of the curtains. When I could finally make out Robert Smith's haunted features on the Cure poster above me, I extracted myself from the warm bed, looked at her peaceful and very beautiful face for the last time, then crept out of the house. Making my way back to the hotel through empty streets, I nervously looked over my shoulder every few yards and almost jumped out of my skin when a startled pigeon flew off noisily.

Time to go home. Well, to London at least.

10 SHOOTING COWS

I had exactly £4.34 in my bank account when I arrived back at Heathrow. No credit card, no overdraft, but luckily, some very kind friends that lent me a bit of money and let me sofa-surf for a couple of months while I found work and saved up for a rental deposit. My parents are wonderful and generous and would have gladly wired me some money if I had asked, but I was too proud to do that. My wages got paid into my account on a Monday, with most going into a savings account that I couldn't get at without writing a formal letter to my bank manager. I withdrew the remaining £50 and that is all I had to cover my living expenses for the week.

Early on, I had to buy some smart shirts for my new job at a publishing company, which left me just £12 to last me through the weekend. I made the mistake of joining my new colleagues for Friday-night drinks and bought a round that completely wiped me out. All I ate that whole weekend was plain boiled rice smothered in ketchup. I wouldn't recommend it.

But life eventually improved as I dragged myself out of poverty. I actually ended up living with Brad, who was also back in London by this time and had rented a big old house in Shepherd's Bush with a couple of South African girls that he knew from Cape Town. We each had a room, then sublet the loft room to a couple of Kiwi blokes who were happy to share to save money. After a week or two, their girlfriends moved in with them, as well as a friend of theirs called Woody. They all slept on mattresses on the floor, which was a bit odd, but we generally got on pretty well, even though the extremely well-bred Cape Town girls didn't approve of the orgy in the attic.

Woody was my favourite. He was an extremely likeable, happy-go-lucky farm boy with, how can I put this, a very healthy sexual appetite. I guess he knew that at the end of the year he would be heading back to his parents' South Island farm for a life of hard work and limited romantic opportunities, and was making hay while the sun shone.

He played the numbers game. He assumed that whenever he went into a bar or club there was at least one lady there who would be receptive to his advances. It was just a matter of finding her, and not letting the many rejections and occasional slaps dent his confidence. He proved his theory correct just about every weekend. You just didn't know who you would meet in the kitchen of a morning, sheepishly making a post-coital cup of tea.

I never quite understood how he did it, even though I witnessed it first-hand on one occasion. We had met for a drink after work in affluent Fulham where Woody was installing a kitchen. We got chatting to a group from a local estate agent, most notably a pretty girl who was rather posh and had done a gap year working in an orphanage in South Africa, and who thought everything about the country was 'stunning'!

We were all getting on very well and I was beginning to think that I might be in with a chance if I played the long game and bought her a G&T or two. I was a bit disappointed when she announced at 9pm that she had to leave to meet up with a friend for dinner. Woody's reply to this news was:

"Oh, I was kind of hoping I could go home with you for a shag!"

My chin hit the floor. I turned to the poor sweet girl to make excuses for my brazen friend, but she quickly replied:

"Oh, okay. In that case, I'll ring my friend to cancel."

I really wasn't getting the hang of this.

Woody got home the following afternoon, grinning like a Cheshire Cat and ever the gentleman, refused to say a word about his evening. The South African girls tutted their disapproval, although funnily enough, Brad let it slip a couple of years later that Woody had been sleeping with one of them all year – creeping down to her room a few nights a week.

But enough of my woeful love life. At least with fishing I enjoyed the occasional success, and I was starting to miss it. London can be a bit of a prison for the economic migrant. You tend to work longer and longer hours, and free time is usually spent in the pub or stretched out in a park somewhere enjoying the tiny bit of sun that you might see every couple of weeks. You force yourself to forget about fishing and concentrate on earning the hard currency that will get you to where the real action is – Alaska, New Zealand, maybe Russia. My naïve perception of the UK's fly fishing is much the same as its cricket – yes sure, it was invented here, but these days, it seems to be much better everywhere else.

In the same vein, would you really want to play golf at St Andrews? Picture the scene – wet, cold Americans shuffling off the last green after shooting 110, going on about history, and tradition and feeling a part of it all – hypothermia and bankruptcy being a small price to pay. When I imagined English fishing, it was either wealthy gentry catching gilt-finned browns on the River Test, or the plebs, one every 10 metres, flogging the water of some marginal put-and-take fishery attempting to catch obese, fin-damaged trout that only yesterday were munching on high-protein pellets in the controlled comfort of the stew pond. In my ignorance, there was nothing in between.

Considering the company that I keep, I shouldn't have been surprised that the water I was invited to fish one weekend was closer to the stew-pond end of the scale. Under normal circumstances I would have refused it, but I was weakened, my fly box hadn't seen the light of day since I had got back from South America several months before, and wonder of wonders, the forecast was for a sunny weekend. To top it off, my work colleague Andrew had been to school with the fishery manager's son and we could fish for free. He assured me that the fishing was excellent: "Like shooting cows in a barn," he said.

Rising earlier than I have on a Saturday morning for many moons, I met Andrew and his brother at the train station and we set off for the 'countryside'. A pleasant half-hour's journey was spent swapping stories, looking through each other's fly boxes, and entertaining the other bemused commuters. Leaving the station, we passed a burger joint, a second-hand car yard garishly decorated with flags, a few cottage shops and then a row of very luxurious houses. A turn to the left, a turn to the right, a few more luxury houses and then we were at the gates of the fishing estate.

To give credit where credit is due, the place was beautiful – immaculately maintained with just the right balance between tradition and convenience. We met the bailiff at the clubhouse, where he served tea and biscuits at no charge. We didn't have to, but the average punter pays £40 and can keep three fish. You are not allowed to release fish and if you catch three in your first three casts, you have to pay another £40 to continue fishing.

We had a look at the hatchery first and I must say that it set my pulse racing. The big-fish pond had monsters up to 20 pounds. It was the first time I had heard the term 'triploid', but the bailiff explained that the fish are bred to be infertile and grow extra fast because no calories are wasted in the reproductive process. I guess they are the fish equivalent of my parents' dog, which had to get de-knackered after wasting too many calories humping visitors' legs.

There wasn't a fisherman every 10 metres. There were about six on the whole lake, which was shaped like a long triangle, about 400 yards long. We made our way to the top end, where a pretty little stream flowed in. The water was crystal clear with long strands of weed swaying in the flow. The keeper had told us that the rainbow trout tended to shoal and success depended on finding a hungry shoal. The water was so clear that we found fish almost straight away.

They were on the bottom in about eight feet of water in the shade of an old wooden boat dock, and there were some big ones. I felt a little ashamed of the carnage that we were about to wreck. I tied a small, weighted Hare's Ear nymph to my 12-foot leader and carefully cast ahead of the main group of fish, letting the current bring the fly to them. They scattered. 10-pound fish scared of a 1cm fly? I tried again with the same result. The shoal moved off and I followed them, changing to a smaller black nymph. They were just as scared of it. I was starting to get frustrated.

There was a whoop from down the bank and Andrew was into a fish on a tiny epoxy buzzer. Not a fly I own. His joy was short lived, as it jumped and spat the hook. It was getting hot and some of the other fishermen were packing it in. I spoke to one of them as he passed me. He said that he was a regular and that in the late summer heat, the fishing seemed to slow right down between 11am and 4pm. I told him about the shoal I had been chasing and he chuckled. Those fish had grown fat on the bread that the owner's kids fed them, and the locals didn't even bother with them. He suggested that I put on a sinking line and try in the deep water off the dam wall. That smacked of patronisation, but I followed his advice when he was out of view down the path.

I had been working hard in the city all week and chucking a sinking line off the dam wall in the stifling midday heat quickly lost any pretence of recreation. I retired to the shade for a while and must have drifted off to sleep. I woke with a start, thinking that one of my companions was trying to drag me feet-first into the lake. It was a massive ram that was aggressively chewing on my shoelaces. I tried kicking it off, but it really liked those laces and followed me down the dam wall to where I could escape over a stile. The day was not turning out how I had envisaged.

I went off to look for the others and found them in deckchairs on the manicured lawn in front of the lodge, enjoying sandwiches and a cold beer. They hadn't had any further success, so we toasted the civilization of the mother country and decided to wait for the cool of afternoon and with any luck, a decent hatch.

I used the time to change back to my floating line and sure enough, at about 4pm, there were a few rises on the edges of the weed beds out in the middle of the lake. A couple of the regulars had reappeared and we watched as they made fantastically long casts, presenting little emergers to the feeding trout, 15 yards further than I could have hoped to reach. It turned out that they had come prepared with seven-weight rods and shooting heads, and I marvelled at the skill required to handle the heavy outfits and still make a delicate presentation. They caught their limits within the hour and we caught nothing. As we made our way back to the train station with our tails between our legs, I reminded Andrew about his 'shooting cows in a barn' simile and silently apologised to the fishing gods for the sins of arrogance, presumption and 'coveting thy neighbour's seven-weight'.

At least we weren't empty handed – the bailiff had given us a few fish from the hatchery to take home for the pot, which Andrew carried in a hemp sack. On the way home, we decided to pop into the White Horse on Parsons Green for a quick pint. One thing led to another and, still carrying our gear and wearing the clothes we had fished in all day, we ended up at a trendy nightclub in nearby Chelsea. The coat room attendant looked a bit bemused when we checked in our rods and fishing jackets, but she refused point-blank to take our sack of trout.

Not wanting to further inhibit our already tainted chances of getting lucky, we left the sack in a dark corner, meaning to recover it later before we went home. Naturally we forgot it, and it seems probable that our only success of the day or night was convincing the nightclub's cleaner of the benefits of catch and release.

11 TARTAN TROUT

"Is this all I get?"

My fellow diner sounded disappointed rather than annoyed, looking down at the plate of steak and chips that the comely Scottish waitress had just delivered. He then leant over to his wife and said, in a loud nasal whisper that American tourists seem prone to, "Do you wanna order something else now, or wait until we've finished this?"

"Let's order now. We don't want to wait too long before we can start shovelling food into our fat gobs again," replied his rotund wife.

Okay, she didn't really, but it wouldn't have surprised me.

I'm in the Scottish Highlands in one of those quaint towns that you see on postcards, quite near that castle that you see on the shortbread tin and in films about dishevelled Scottish guys with odd accents throwing off the yoke of English suppression. What's more, I'm not alone. I'm with a girl. I met her in London, which isn't that notable, you could meet a girl every three feet in London, though they would think you a little strange. Rachel is actually from Bristol in the West of England and was only visiting the capital for the weekend. In other words, she hasn't met many South Africans, hasn't been burned by one of my notoriously cavalier countrymen and, despite the dire warnings from her London friends, has actually been willing to give me a chance.

It has been a long-distance relationship so far, and this is our first holiday together. The first time that we have spent more than two days in a row together, the first time I have seen Rachel read a map, or not read a map, as the case may be. I'm on my best behaviour. I've brought a fly rod and have been itching to fish in Scotland for years, to catch my first truly wild trout, but I haven't been brave enough to broach the subject yet. She knows that I'm South African, that I am lacking in sophistication, can only cook on an open fire and only wear shoes when I really, really have to. But it's just too soon for her to find out about the whole feral fisherman thing.

I am one-eighth Scottish. I have got a great grandfather who was 5' 2", ginger; and had a close affinity with his country's alcoholic exports. A few things started to make sense when I found that out. I don't know if the tenuous ancestral linkage entitles me to wear a kilt, but it might explain the urge that I have always felt to visit this place. To be perfectly honest, as a holiday destination, it takes patience. It has rained every day that we have been here, although we have had an hour or two here and there where the sun has managed to poke through the mizzle. But I like it – it is atmospheric and you can always get away from the American coach tours by heading ever further north. We went right to the top, where you can look out to sea and on a clear day see polar bears floating around on icebergs. Not exactly – but it certainly feels that way.

The main road up there is a single track – and by that I don't mean a single track each way. There is only space for one car, so you have to keep pulling over to navigate past various disgruntled locals and other intrepid tourists. You quickly learn to multitask – keeping an eye on the road, taking in the fantastic scenery and eating another piece of chocolate shortbread all at the same time. It is truly beautiful: in every direction are mountains, rushing salmon rivers and picturesque lochs. Though make sure you don't call them 'lakes' when asking directions from grumpy farmers.

I read somewhere once that the Scottish average for salmon is one fish per angler per week. That's pretty sobering, but when you marry it to the other well-known statistic, that five per cent of the anglers catch 95 per cent of the fish, and you begin to wonder if perhaps it would have been more productive to have stayed at home and bought antique fly rods on eBay. I have always wanted to try it, though, even to say that I have, and to give myself the slightest chance of catching one. This wasn't the time and place, though, and I would be more than happy if I could just catch a truly wild trout.

Now don't get me wrong, if I was on a proper fishing trip I would sell the old girl to get a few days' salmon fishing. By 'old girl' I mean my rusty van, in case you were thinking I was mad enough to refer to my lovely new girlfriend in those terms. This was a couple holiday after all, and even I know that sitting in a car next to some frigid river is not the best way to melt a girl's heart.

Normally, I'm not that keen on a stolen afternoon's fishing. I'll take one any chance I get, but it's just not the same as trips that have been long in planning and sweet in anticipation – where you've read all the guide books and have tied enough flies for the bag-search guy at the airport to give you a very funny look.

I grabbed my opportunity when it came. Rachel mentioned that she had some present shopping to do and wouldn't mind a couple of hours on her own to make the rounds of the gift shops. Feigning hurt feelings because she didn't want to spend every waking hour with me, I said that I was happy to entertain myself – go for a walk, or maybe go fishing or something. In a flash, I was down at the local tackle shop interrogating the poor owner about what fishing was on offer. I was hoping to get a beat on one of the local brown-trout streams, but I was to be disappointed. With the recent rain, they were all in spate and unfishable. A loch would have to do.

The local fishing club leased day tickets on local lochs for a very reasonable £6. The guy in the shop told me that they were never stocked and held a self-sufficient population of wild brown trout that spawned in the feeder streams. There was even the chance of a Ferox trout, which I always thought were a separate species, until I learnt that they are simply large brown trout that turn cannibalistic and feed on fry in the depths. There was a stuffed one on the wall, caught locally and weighing 16 pounds.

The loch I decided on was 20 minutes' drive from town, on a plateau overlooking the sea. It's a strange feeling tackling up for a spot of trout fishing with the sea just below you, especially when it's sunny and warm as the day had turned out to be.

I had a look at my fly box and was absolutely stumped. All the flies for sale in the tackle shop had been winged traditional patterns – Invictas, Connemara Blacks and so on. I'm not sure about you, but I have a huge mental block when it comes to the classic old flies. I think it stems from all the barren days I had using them as a youngster. I'm sure that in the right hands, they can be very effective, but unfortunately, those hands are attached to someone else's arms.

I had a couple of big streamers and Woolly Buggers left over from Patagonia, but I was reluctant to use them. I was after a truly wild trout and, although I have as much claim to purism as Madonna has to virginity, I wanted to catch one the proper way. I settled on two small nymphs, a greenish one and a brownish one, and began fishing the shallow water in a bay near the car park. The water was that whisky colour typical of the peaty highlands and there was an interesting-looking scum line where the wind-ruffled open water started.

After half an hour with no interest, I turned over a couple of stones in the shallows, but there was no life except for a couple of tiny grubby things. There were a few terrestrials floating in the scum line, but I hadn't seen any rises and I'm not the biggest fan of fishing dry flies blind on still water.

I walked around the loch, which was amoeba shaped and about half a mile across at its widest point. I found a small feeder stream that rushed off the rocky hillside and spilled into a small bay. I changed the point fly to a skinny Black Buzzer and then to a bigger Hare's Ear nymph that I managed to catch in the heather behind me, causing a huge tangle. It was while sitting on a rock untangling the mess that I saw a shoal of little minnows in the shallows. I cut off the bird's nest and put thoughts of purity to the back of my mind. On went a fat Marabou Streamer, which I lobbed out, at last with a bit of confidence.

Half an hour of casting and the confidence was just about dry. At least I saw a rise, but it was way out in the bay, far out of range. I was running out of time now. My desire to catch a wild Scottish trout was not as strong as my desire to maintain a harmonious relationship. I had a last look through my fly box and my eye stopped on a couple of shaggy black flies that I hadn't used for ages. Something that Tom Sutcliffe once wrote came back to me. This was a long time ago, but he said that if he was only allowed to fish one fly anywhere in the world, it would be a Black Woolly Worm. I had nothing to lose, so I tied on a medium-sized one, moved along the bay a bit and threw the longest cast I could manage. I had just started a steady retrieve when I got that beautiful handshake and was into my first ever, genuine, so-wild-my-ancestors-evolved-here, brown trout. It wasn't very big, but it still counted. Thank you Tom Sutcliffe!

Walking hand in hand to the pub that night, a picture of domestic bliss, the rain started to fall again and didn't stop for the last four days of our holiday. There is a good saying in Scotland that there is no such thing as bad weather, just unsuitable clothing. With this in mind, we took to the misty hills in our fleeces and waterproofs and finished off what was an excellent 10-day break – and you wouldn't usually hear me say that when I've only caught one small trout.

12 MY HEART BELONGS IN NEMPNETT THRUBWELL

After a year of weekend commuting between London and Bristol, it was decided that I would leave the bustle and hectic pace of London for the relative tranquillity of the West Country. Surrounded by lakes, rivers and cows, I felt at home immediately.

Adjusting to the human locals was a bit more challenging. Even if you have never set foot in the West Country, or even the UK, you would instantly recognise the accent. Think pirates. I'm not sure where it started, but pirates in popular culture always speak with a Bristolian accent. This may date back to the infamous Blackbeard, who was apparently a man called Edward Teach, born near the Bristol docks around 1680. History doesn't record if he said "Arrrrrr!" at the start of every sentence.

Leaving the city and heading out into the countryside of Somerset and Gloucestershire, the accent morphs into a softer, lilting burr that you will also recognise. Somewhat unfairly, it is often used to represent rural simpletons or other yokels. That seems a tad unfair to me, though the locals seem to embrace it. Bristol and surrounding areas almost always tops the 'happiest place in the UK' polls and the people are warm and generous folk, who don't really give a carrot what fancy Londoners think of them.

To be honest, my problem was not me understanding them, it was the other way round. It seems that while London is full of South Africans, not many of us had infiltrated the cider belt, and people were not used to my flat vowels and strange idioms. I had to get used to repeating myself, or speaking very slowly and being careful not to loudly ask for 'arse in ma drink' when ordering in a busy pub.

Speaking of pubs, there have been some other adjustments to make. Having grown up with South Africa's service industry, which was mostly bored or surly, or sometimes both, it came as a very pleasant surprise to find that in the UK, bar staff, shop assistants and even petrol station night staff are generally both efficient and friendly. They even use terms of endearment that I had only ever heard from my mother. I first experienced it in London. Walking into any pub in the city you would most likely get "Alright darlin'? Watcha havin''?" Or possibly 'mate' if it was a bloke behind the bar, though not necessarily, especially in the Soho area.

In the more genteel suburbs, you will get called 'my dear' a lot, and on a work trip to Leeds in the North of England, I had a comedic interaction with a hotel receptionist who I thought had mistaken me for another guest called Pete. It turned out she was asking "Is there anything else I can do for you, pet?

Darling, love, pet and even duck – these charming terms of affection leave you with a fuzzy glow after every encounter. However, in Bristol, they go for something that bit more intimate, and the warm glow is most likely the blush of my profound embarrassment. I first heard it when visiting Rach for the first time. Being the classy guy that I am, I was treating her to a fry-up in a local greasy-spoon café on Saturday morning. When taking my order, the septuagenarian waitress asked "Would you like any sauce with that, my lover?" My lover! I was never expecting to be called that, especially by someone as old as my grandmother, with slightly more facial hair than my grandfather. I've been called it countless times since and have never got used to it.

Rachel finds my cultural floundering hilarious. She is from solid Bristol working-class stock, but as a Paralegal at a top law firm, she can shift effortlessly from dealing with skinhead scaffolders with facial tattoos to plummy attorneys called Tarquin who play polo on the weekend.

I might just be her biggest challenge, though. She has gradually come to realise exactly what she has let herself in for. The pile of fishing magazines was the first clue, the neoprene waders stinking out her shed the second. It was a bit of a shock for her when I first unpacked my fly-tying kit, especially the Hare's Mask, but she came to accept my passion as one of the cultural nuances that make cohabitation with a foreigner interesting.

One nuance that she wasn't very thrilled to discover was that I was a very typical South African male when it came to domestic experience. I had to put that right in a hurry – learning how a vacuum cleaner works, how to iron clothes and that you aren't supposed to wash red socks and expensive white underwear together. I even learnt how to cook indoors, in an actual oven rather than on an open fire. I felt extremely proud of myself.

When I wasn't smashing gender stereotypes in the kitchen, I started to dip my toe in the vast amount of fishing that I now had on my doorstep. I was amazed that just about every little stream in the area held a few trout, even those running through urban areas. Sure, there was the occasional shopping trolley and traffic cone, but the water quality must have been excellent as the fish were very happy. On my lunch hour one day, I even saw some little brown trout living in a storm drain on the side of a busy road. God knows how they got there, but they seemed to be thriving and rose confidently to the bits of my baguette that I threw in for them.

When it comes to lakes, I really hit the jackpot. The nearest one is rather famous and is only 15 minutes' drive away in the shadow of the gorgeous Mendip Hills. If you get a bit lost on the way there, you might pass little villages that seem straight out of Jane Austin – Pucklechurch, Chew Magna and my personal favourite, Nempnett Thrubwell.

Blagdon Lake was first opened in 1904 and has been called the home of stillwater fishing in the UK. It has a handsome mock-Tudor lodge and is set in scenery that is quintessentially English. Many of the flies and tactics that we take for granted were first developed there, and fly fishers from all over the UK and Europe regard it with a certain reverence. I really had picked the right girlfriend.

It is big lake at about 440 acres, although it is smaller than its big brother Chew Valley Lake that is only another two miles away, which is also stocked with trout. There are about four kilometres of bank fishing, or you can hire one of the wooden boats that have a small petrol engine. It really is top-drawer fishing. It isn't cheap, but you can fish from an hour before sunrise to an hour after sunset, which in mid-summer gives you about 18 hours on a day ticket. Not bad value, even to a South African that is still subconsciously converting every price into humble Rands.

With the season opening a couple of weeks ago, I haven't had the best start so far. In three outings, I haven't actually landed a single trout by conventional methods. A feisty two-pounder gave me a fantastic fight, but broke my heart when it slipped into the net backwards, the Green Buzzer hooked firmly through its back. I told myself that it was probably going for the fly and missed, but for some reason, that didn't ease the pain.

With the lake full of the new season stock fish, others have done very well, and I've had to watch them fill their boots while I blanked. I am not used to fishing with other people that I don't know. In South Africa, I was lucky enough to have access to some excellent private and club water, where you would feel a bit peeved if you spotted another angler on your lake. Not so at Blagdon. On opening day the wind was blowing hard from the north, so all anglers were crammed on the windward bank. This meant that I had to find a place to squeeze in, and had someone 20 metres on either side of me, and then every 20 metres along the entire length of the lake. The latecomers had to side-cast across the wind, or into its teeth on the opposite bank.

Everyone else wades, some dangerously deep for their advanced years, so I had to join them to access clear water. Aquatic insect life is tiny compared to South African lakes and it seems you need to use a team of size 12 or 14 buzzers or nymphs and inch them back as slowly as possible. It got a bit tedious, to be honest. I couldn't move as all the other good spots were taken, and there was absolutely no action in my section of water. But no matter, the countryside was beautiful and the old geezer on my left told me that he has been fishing Blagdon for 40 years and that the fish don't really start feeding until the shallows warm up towards mid-morning, but you have to be there by 7am to get a place.

At just after 11, I heard a splash off to my left and someone down the line was into a fish. Then the next rod in the row bent over and so it continued as the shoal made its way down the bank. I waited in fervent anticipation for my turn, but there must have been something wrong as my rod remained straight and the action carried on to my right, before it all went quiet again; the only noise being the occasional thump of the priest as the first fish of the season were dispatched and slipped into creels.

One good thing about a busy lake is that you get to talk to a lot of people. The locals are incredibly friendly and it is common for someone to give you a few flies if you haven't got the right ones. I even had a guy bite off the fly that he had just caught a fish on and hand it over. Embarrassingly, I lost it in the grass behind me 10 minutes later, but I was still very touched.

I have also learnt about tactics and setups that I had never considered before. The lake shelves gently so you are never fishing into very deep water. The standard rig seems to be a floating line with a team of three flies on about a 16-foot leader – you try casting that in a wind and you will get very good at untangling knots. The main food source for the trout on Blagdon is chironomids, also called 'buzzers' due to the sound they make when they take to the air in numbers.

The most successful flies imitate the slim pupal stage when the little creatures rise from the mud and hang in the water column prior to hatching, where they are easy pickings for the roving trout. Black or green seem to be the most popular colours in the early season, some with a bit of flash in them and others with white antron at the head to represent the breathers that are so obvious on the spent shucks that litter the surface after a hatch.

If things are slow, then you might put a little mini lure on the end – black and bright green again seems to be a popular colour combination – but apparently, it is a last resort and "not really cricket", according to one of the old gents that I spoke to, who bore an uncanny resemblance to the deaf Major from Fawlty Towers.

Another rig is what is called a 'wash line'. It was shown to me by a giant of a man who waded out next to me in Rugmoor Bay one evening and proceeded to catch four fish in four casts after I had been flogging the water fruitlessly for two hours. He must have noticed my inquisitive looks as he explained that the fish were high in the water and I needed to "hang out the washing". In a rich Somerset accent, he explained that it is a three-fly rig on a long leader with a floating Booby on the point, and two flies on droppers. If you can imagine a long washing line – sagging in the middle with two little buzzers hanging down – it makes a lot of sense. Straight nymphs would fish too deep in these situations. He tied up a new cast while I watched, his big sausage fingers showing amazing dexterity as he finished the whole lot in about a minute – in the wind, no less. Although to be fair, he had the wind-blocking attributes of a barn.

You get pike in Blagdon, too. I haven't seen or caught any yet, but the lake record is over 40 pounds. The guy in the office was telling me that he hooked one of 28 pounds on a nymph while fishing for trout. It took him 30 minutes to land and it put a permanent bend in his six-weight. Pike are native to England, but seem a bit out of place in the pastoral tranquillity, with their jagged dentistry and voracious feeding habits. I tell you, if I was wading and a 40-pound pike swam by, I would make very sure that I was in no deeper than my middle thigh, if you get my drift.

The best bit about Blagdon is that being so close, on a summer evening I can leave work and still have five hours' fishing in beautiful surroundings, before domestic duties call. I'm bound to catch something sooner or later, aren't I?

Even if I don't, Nempnett Thrubwell is just lovely this time of year, my lover.

13 ITCHY FEET

Seeing as I had only intended moving to the UK for a year to earn money and soak up the excitement of London, it came as a bit of a surprise to friends and family that five years later I was still here, living a life of comfortable domesticity in the West Country, with an actual woman. Given my romantic track record, I was somewhat surprised myself.

But something was amiss. I considered myself very lucky to have met Rachel and our settled life in Bristol was infinitely better than my chaotic single life in London, but I knew that there were decisions to be made in the future and that the life path I had always imagined for myself was going to take a few twists and turns. In the back of my mind, I always thought I would travel the world but end up back in South Africa. I missed the wildness, the vibrancy, the possibility of adventure around every corner. In some ways, I was still that mud-caked boy crawling under a barbed-wire fence to fish a mysterious lake that may have held the fish of my dreams. I didn't realise it, but in much more important ways, I wasn't that boy anymore. I just wasn't ready to see it yet.

I took Rachel back to South Africa for a holiday and to meet my family. She absolutely loved it and the family loved her. I'm pretty sure they had thought I was a lost cause in the romance department, and I swear my mum kept touching her, not out of affection, but to make sure she was real. I think I was also subconsciously holding Rachel up to the African backdrop, to see if she matched, if we could ever live there. To be honest, I wasn't even sure that I could anymore.

While we were passing through Cape Town, we were invited around to my cousin's house for the South African ritual of day drinking and cremating obscene amounts of meat – the braai. There were a few other couples there in their mid-20s and within 10 minutes, the men were shirtless in the pool drinking beer and telling rude jokes while the immaculately dressed WAGs were in the kitchen making salad, talking about soft furnishings and how much they paid their cleaners.

Rach uneasily joined in the kitchen W.I. meeting, but would definitely have preferred to be in the pool. Over lunch, when the conversation moved on to which private school the as-yet-unconceived children would be attending, Rach flashed me a look that I understood 100 per cent. We didn't stay long, and I was quite relieved when we went back to the UK a couple of days later, where our friends didn't behave like characters from a US soap opera.

That holiday didn't make everything clear immediately, but it set a few wheels in motion. Of course, I hadn't mentioned any of my uncertainty to Rachel, as I was terrified that she would misunderstand and give me the hoof. There was no version of the life I wanted that didn't include her, I just didn't know the details yet.

I didn't plan any of it. We were away for a weekend of walking in the country, and over a nice bottle of red wine in an old Cotswold pub, the conversation got onto where in the world we would still like to travel to. We had never actually discussed it before. Rach had done a lot of travelling before we met and had lived in Australia for a year, so I assumed that she had got it out of her system and wanted to settle down. For my part, I had never mentioned any travel desires as I didn't want her to think I was that kiss-and-run Saffa that her London friends had warned about.

It was like floodgates opening. I had never seen Rach so enthusiastic about anything that didn't have a cork in it. Firstly, she hadn't seen any of the wild West Coast of Australia, had always wanted to work on a farm in New Zealand, and then she reeled off a list of exotic countries in South East Asia that I had definitely heard of, but could not confidently point out on a map... probably due to their hot climates and lack of trout. I was up for all of it, though.

We hatched some plans. We rented out Rach's flat, I cashed in some of my London savings and we spent a good three hours in the travel agent with a very patient man called Duncan finalising our itinerary. I'm not a total idiot, this wasn't going to be a repeat of South America. We planned, we budgeted, we got up-to-date information from friends and a wonderful new invention called the internet. We applied for work visas for New Zealand and joined a scheme there where you can exchange work on farms for bed and board. We were more prepared than I had ever been for anything. That didn't stop me having a small panic attack when I quit my job and paid for my open-ended air ticket.

With nine months in New Zealand, of course I was taking some fly rods, but this was not going to be a feral trip by any means. I can't help it if feral things just happen to me.

14 SALTWATER HERO

I am not a saltwater fly fisherman. I have tried, but I don't think it is meant to be. I haven't got the titanium-reinforced fingers, the Clint Eastwood stare, and I am rubbish at casting in the wind. I haven't caught much either, and I'm not being modest when I say that. An anorexic cat would starve to death if it had to live off my catch. I once landed a couple of shad at Kosi Bay, assorted junk in Durban harbour and I once hooked something substantial while trolling off a kayak on the Natal South Coast, which might have towed me to Madagascar if the line hadn't snapped.

If it wasn't for two evenings' fishing at Coral Bay on the Ningaloo Reef in the far North West of Australia, I would deny having ever picked up an eight-weight. If you haven't heard of the Ningaloo Reef, don't worry, I hadn't either before we started researching our trip. The reason it is relatively unknown and almost completely unspoilt is that it is very, very far away from anywhere. The closest city is Perth; about 1,500 dusty dry kilometres to the south, and the major centres of Sydney and Melbourne are over 4,000 kilometres away through the red centre of the country. A lot of Aussies haven't heard of it, either!

Unlike its big brother, the Great Barrier Reef on the other side of the continent, the Ningaloo can be reached by swimming off the beach and at many places, by just wading a few feet offshore. Looking at the map is an adventure in itself. The region is filled with wonderfully evocative names: Shark Bay, Coral Bay and Monkey Mia seem right out of a pirate story.

The Shark Bay tourist authority would be far happier if they could change the name of the town to something like 'Pretty Beach' or 'Azure

Bay'. Its tourist guide assures the holidaymaker that Shark Bay is no sharkier than any of the places along the coast, but I'm not too sure about that. It was named by William Dampier in 1699, whose crew noticed an extraordinarily large number of sharks when they moored in the bay on their way south. And if you think things have changed since then, we met a charming old guy in the local bar who said that he swims every morning and only the previous week, had been bumped by a large tiger shark. Now he swims a little closer to shore.

Coral Bay is a little way up the coast (only 400km) and I'm fairly sure its tourist authority is in constant ecstasy. There isn't much to it. A hotel, a backpacker's hostel, a couple of fishing and dive charters and the most exquisite stretch of beach that you have ever sunk your toes into. White sand, blue water and the Ningaloo Reef literally a left-handed stone's throw off the beach. We went snorkelling on the day we arrived and, following the dive shop's advice, walked a kilometre or so down the beach, swam out to the reef and then let the slight current carry us back to the sheltered bay that is a marine reserve.

I have done a bit of snorkelling in South Africa and Mauritius and this beat it hands down. The coral was the colours you are expecting from watching those nature programmes, and there were hundreds of fish of every colour you could imagine. After 10 minutes, I heard a squeal underwater and turned to see Rachel pointing excitedly at a turtle gliding past us, with that look of disdain that turtles seem permanently fixed with.

I was thinking about my fly-rods back at the hostel and was on the lookout for game fish, but all the life seemed delicate and pretty rather than large and fast. After two hours of underwater sightseeing, we drifted into the bay and the start of the marine reserve. There was no barrier or anything like that and the only indication was a faded old sign on the beach that instructed beach goers that fishing or anchoring of boats was not allowed in the reserve.

Australia has to be the most law-abiding country in the world. Even on the remote desert roads, with no bends, let alone police on the road, no one drives over the 100km limit. If you do, you can expect a hoot and a finger shaking from anyone that you pass. So the marine reserve was as untouched as Chuck Norris' daughter and it showed right away. A snapper looks a bit like a steenbras and is a sought-after game fish in

Australia. The further we got into the reserve, the bigger they seemed to get, completely unphased by us, 20 or 30 pounds of prime eating, fining nonchalantly by. That got me a bit twitchy.

One of the fishing charters also sold a bit of tackle – no flies, but they did have a few casting spoons and rubber shrimps and the guy behind the counter said that he had seen people fly fishing on the edge of the reserve. He advised me to try at sunset and after and be prepared for anything. He hadn't heard of snapper being caught on fly, but trevally and barracuda would take a lure, so theoretically, a fly as well.

I was more than a little excited now. I walked up the beach a couple of hours early and waded out so that a full cast would drop the fly in about eight feet of water, just where the coral started. I cast and cast with a flashabou streamer, changed to a shrimp, then to a popper and back to a streamer when my stripping arm started getting sore. The only interest I had was from people walking along the beach, who stopped to watch and take the piss out of me, in the Australian tradition.

The sun started to set and Rachel came down the beach and made me pose for a couple of photographs with the ever-more-impressive sunset in the background. She had a few casts with my rod, without hooking me or herself, or a fish for that matter, which was good for the relationship. It was a glorious evening, a slight warm wind blew offshore and I was very content, even though my enthusiasm for fishing had long since waned.

Then off to our right, right up against the shore – a tell-tale splash and the shimmer of little baitfish fleeing something toothy. The enthusiasm was back in a flash and the casting lesson came to an abrupt end. I cast in the general direction of the commotion and stripped the fly back in. I cast again a bit deeper with the same result, and then again. I was beginning to think it was a one-off when there was a shower of spray and hundreds of little fish shot out of the water all around us, even between us and the shore.

Rachel screamed! This wasn't the sedate trout fishing that she was used to. The baitfish seemed to be using us as shelter and swarmed all around our legs. That was enough for Rach and she splashed back to the safety of the beach. I carried on casting, but still had no takes. I seemed to have picked exactly the right place, though. I had chosen it because it was closest to the coral, but as the tide flooded in, it formed a little bay that the predators seemed to be herding the baitfish into.

The light was fading fast, but there was still activity all around me. Rachel had had enough and was heading back along the beach when there was a snatch on my line. I hadn't been retrieving when it hit – I had been admiring Rach's retreating figure. I was very interested to find out what had been tormenting me. It wasn't huge, but it was lively and gave my eight-weight a real workout. I beached it and found it was a juvenile trevally, what we would call a Kingfish in South Africa. Only about 30cm in length, it was already showing the brutish body shape that would be snapping fly rods in a couple of years.

I cast out again, retrieving just fast enough to stop the fly sinking to the bottom. Again, the fly was snatched by a trevally, which somersaulted out of the water, spitting it out in the process. This was fun. The next cast was also taken, but this was something different. It felt a lot heavier and fought more like a big brown trout, lots of head knocking but not too many fireworks.

It swam me around for five minutes before I caught a glimpse of it. It looked like I had hooked a supersize cricket bat – it was long and narrow, but quite deep bodied. I guessed that it was some sort of barracuda, but didn't study it too hard with its thrashing tail and impressive set of teeth. I was just happy to extract the fly without spilling any blood.

The streamer was completely mangled, though, like it had been plugged into the mains. The only similar fly that I had was blue and silver, and quite a bit bigger. I'm not sure what possessed me to first buy it – I certainly wasn't going marlin fishing. I eventually got it tied on in the gloom, and laid out a short cast in front of me – not expecting a take but daydreaming of the next day's headline in the Coral Bay Express (readership 16): 'Fly-Fisherman Catches Record Trevally'.

I soon hooked something, but it was no record – I was amazed the little trevally had opened its mouth wide enough to get its mouth around the gape of the hook! I got lots more takes after that, but none of them had the same mouth-stretching ability. I reluctantly headed back to the hostel in the pitch dark, still an unknown fly fisherman with a giant fly, yelping every few seconds as I stood on sharp and unseen bits of coral.

The next evening, after an exciting day tearing down the beach on a quad bike, I was back at the inlet. This time with a torch, a couple of Bucktail Streamers, and a German. The torch I had bought in the dive shop, the flies I had tied hurriedly that afternoon and the German I had picked up in the hostel, because he wanted to try casting a fly. He bought along his bait-casting rod as well, which is just as well because I wasn't that keen on spending my last night in Coral Bay giving casting lessons.

On cue, just after sunset, the first of the splashes started. The German hadn't much liked fly-casting and I think he felt a lot more confident with the chunk of bait that he lobbed out into the channel. The activity was even more frenetic than the night before, but unfortunately, my Bucktail Streamers weren't as attractive as I'd hoped. I left them still, I twitched them and I stripped them through the commotion, all with no result. I thought it might because they lacked flash, and changed to a small Crazy Charlie, but that was useless because it sank straight to the shallow bottom.

There was nothing else for it, it was back on with the yard-of-fly, the big blue and silver streamer. Almost right away it was attacked, my rod ducked and jerked like a water diviner's rod in a flood, but nothing stuck. The German thought it was very funny. I thought he smelt bad.

Then amazingly, it was his rod that bucked. He started yelling and whooping as something strong throbbed on the end of the line. He kept it up for five minutes and there was a small crowd around us when he eventually landed a big Snapper. I have never seen such a proud fisherman before, or for that matter a happier German.

He tied on another chuck of bait and joined me again in the thigh-deep water on the edge of the bay. It was still light enough to see the splashes, but not enough to actually see into the water. Then the German pointed out a patch of water that looked a little strange. It was about 10 metres away and the size of a large dining-room table. It was darker than the water around it and seemed to be moving very slowly towards us.

My first thought was that it was a densely packed shoal of fish. We watched it mesmerised for a moment before my companion made a dash for the beach, yelling "Scheisse, scheisse, scheisse!" That rattled me for a second and I also backed towards the sand, keeping an eye on the shadow that passed like a ghost under my rod tip. We realised later that it must have been a very large but harmless manta ray, but when you are near a place called Shark Bay, you don't take any chances.

I would like to say that my next cast yielded an Australian record trevally and that I was carried back to town on the shoulders of an excited throng of fly-fishing converts. In reality, it was just me and the German making our weary way back along a very pretty stretch of beach, happy and smelling faintly of fish.

15 RAISING COWS

I'm not sure that sheep wrestling is something that I will put on my CV, but after our time working on a farm in New Zealand, I am 100 per cent qualified.

It sounded perfect – the website said that you only had to work four or five hours a day on the farm to get full board and lodging in return. It went on to say that duties might include gardening, cleaning, and perhaps some light farm work. That sounded good, I reckoned I could scatter a bit of chicken feed or bail a bit of hay.

Rachel and I had spent an amazing six weeks in Australia, almost a month in a New Zealand ski resort, but now we had a few months to kill before the height of summer when were planning to see the rest of New Zealand and then go overland from Bali to Bangkok. We couldn't afford to break into our savings, so working on a farm seemed like a perfect way to get a true taste of the country and not spend any money. It was just a bonus that in rural New Zealand you can't walk far without sloshing through some classic stretch of trout stream.

It was so easy; we emailed the farm that sounded the best for us and we got an email back the same day saying that we could start the following week – I had to remind myself that this was New Zealand, where everything works, where bureaucracy is left to the bureaucrats and hard farm work is left to... well, to Rachel and me, apparently.

Bannockburn Farm, owned by Barb and Stuart McPherson, is located in a picturesque valley in the South Canterbury region of the South Island. Barb's email said that they had sheep (of course, this is New Zealand after all), a couple hundred bullocks and deer. She offered to pick us up from the bus station, but I assured her that Bertha, our trusty 1983 Toyota station wagon (bought for the princely sum of £400) would get us there. She also said that they had lots of 'fun things' for us to do at the moment, as their labourer had recently left and they were a bit busier than usual. That is when I should have smelt a rat. It was a 2,000-acre farm, didn't she mean 'one of their many labourers had recently left'?

We arrived and met Barb and Stuart. Barb was your typical friendly, salt-of-the earth farm girl and Stuart the original strong-silent type. We also met their six dogs, two cats and a couple of pigs called Ping and Pong. Stuart was in the middle of inoculating 350 sheep by himself, and I quickly realised that there was no legion of labourers – it was just Barb and Stuart, and now us.

Barb found us some overalls and wellies and our first job was to help her take two of the heavily pregnant sheep down to a lower paddock and help her give them a glucose injection. She suspected that they were carrying triplets and the poor dears just couldn't eat enough grass to keep up with their demands, leaving them lethargic and in danger of starving. Two sheep regrettably became one, as one of them banged her head on the side of the trailer, had a heart attack and promptly dropped dead at our feet.

Rachel and I exchanged worried looks, we fancied that we weren't your average soft city types, but this wasn't the start we were expecting. Unfortunately, a deceased sheep was just the beginning.

Barb drove us down to the paddock with us on the back of the quad bike and one live and one dead sheep bouncing along in the trailer behind. She explained that it should be quite simple to inject the remaining sheep, as it was sapped of energy and wouldn't put up much of a struggle. We got it out of the trailer and had to ease her onto her back for the injection, so that her unborn lambs were not damaged. In retrospect, I think this is when the poor ewe caught sight of the industrial-size syringe that Barb was about to stick her with. She suddenly had all the energy of an All Black doing the haka, and began kicking and bucking.

"Jump on it, jump on it!" yelled Barb, as soft city types Dave and Rachel went flying into the mud. I jumped on the sheep, finding that her woolly pelt offered a firm grip. I managed to twist her around so that she was sitting on her bum, half on my lap with her legs in the air.

Barb managed to inject her and she bolted off, but not before Stone Cold Dave Hitchins had pinned her for the three-count.

Okay, I was getting into this farming lark. The next job was to feed the bullocks. That sounded more like what I was expecting. Only that the bullocks were pretty much full size and feeding them was not just a matter of chucking some feed into a trough. Grass doesn't grow too well in the winter and hay is expensive, so what Stuart had done is grow a few fields of a feed crop that looked a little like giant cabbage and a lot like it could take over the world, like in The Day Of The Triffids.

The bullocks start at one end of the field with a movable electric fence separating them from the crops, which they would trample into the mud in no time if they had the run of the whole field. A daily job was to move the electric fence by one metre so that the bullocks would have a metre-long strip of feed to munch on every day. Now bullocks are not the brightest of creatures, but if this happens every day, they soon realise that to move the fence you have to switch the electric current off, and once that is done, a puny little fence is no barrier when there is a whole field of food to be had.

My job was to get them back into their portion of the field while Rachel and Barb moved the fence. If there had been a video camera there, you would be seeing me on next week's 'Funniest Farm Videos'. Running through waist-high cabbage is not easy, but add to that the mud, the wild gesticulating and trying to figure out what to shout… you had to shout something to get their attention, and 'yee-haa' sounded a bit too American, handclapping a bit too camp. I wasn't about to shout 'moooo-ve', in case I was mistaken for a nubile young cow. I settled for a loud 'G'it!', which Barb found very funny. She just swore at them.

We eventually got it done and I was looking forward to getting back to the farmhouse, getting clean, having a large cup of tea and maybe even unpacking! It was not to be. Stuart had finished inoculating the sheep and a huge triple-decker truck had arrived to take them an hour down the valley to some pastures that he was leasing. We had to help get them loaded. The dogs did most of the work, herding them through a funnel, but it was our job to get them up the ramp, which was not easy once we had got to the truck's upper level and the ramp was quite steep.

The dogs got a bit too enthusiastic at times, nipping at heels and panicking the sheep so that they tried to climb over each other to get up the ramp. This tactic went wrong for one ewe that was forced over the side of the ramp in the melee. This would have been a six-foot drop to the ground and probable injury. "Catch it!" roared Stuart and I was unfortunately the person closest. It landed on my head and the world went black for a second, my face stuffed into its smelly, woolly side. I managed to manhandle it back over the fence and it bolted up into the truck without a word of thanks.

Okay – we had to have a break now. I think we were actually about to. Even Stuart looked tired. But then he noticed that one of the dogs had a nasty gash on its leg that would have to be stitched. Naturally, it was the biggest one, a beast that looked like a cross between a Rottweiler and a horse. Barb drove and I had to hold the dog still for the 15km bumpy ride into town. Now you have to know something about me – I am possibly the most squeamish person ever. I once passed out watching a childbirth documentary on the Discovery Channel. If the blood is mine, then it is no problem, but someone else's or an animal's and someone better be around to catch me.

I held the front end of the dog, which luckily hadn't seemed to have noticed its injury, and looked out the window. We got to the vet with no major incident – most importantly, the dog hadn't bitten me. The vet decided that stitches were needed and someone had to hold the animal while these were done – yep, another job for the South African. I was beginning to regret that World Cup win.

To be fair, the dog was completely unphased by the whole experience. It looked around like a child at Disney World, taking in all the exciting sights and smells and licking my face whenever I got close enough.

That was the first afternoon and I am pleased to say that it got easier after that – or we toughened up really quickly, it's difficult to say. We slipped into the rhythms of the farm day, which began with feeding the new calves at 8am. Every day they seemed bigger and stronger than the day before. Feeding 120 calves is a lot more difficult than it sounds. The powdered milk had to be mixed in huge vats and stirred by hand, with just the right ratios. Too much powder and you have got 120 calves with the runs, too little and they won't grow at the optimum rate.

With 10 calves to a pen, they are fed by pouring the milk into a segmented trough with 10 teats on it. As soon as you do this, there is a stampede of starving calves and it was Rachel's job to make sure that each calf got its own teat. They look sweet and all, but when they have got their lips latched to lunch, they find hidden reserves of strength, which makes shifting them a difficult task. Luckily, dealing with stubborn hungry males is a speciality of Rachel's, and her calves were soon lined up like skittles, sucking away and flicking their tails in ecstasy.

Now if you just ate lunch yourself, you might want to skip the next bit of the story. The best way of gauging the health of a calf is – and there is no nice way of saying this – to check the colour and consistency of its poo. The best time to do this is when all the calves are lined up at the feeding trough and this is when poor Rachel had to do it. I was excused because my muscles were needed to shift heavy milk troughs, so she had to go from calf to calf, lifting their tails and making sure that all was as it should be. Another skill for the CV.

As spring arrived, it slowly warmed and the jobs on the farm changed, the snow on the hills started to melt and everywhere life started bursting from every nook and crevice. We worked outside a lot, digging a new vegetable garden, building retaining walls and new paddocks for the deer. When it rained, we fixed the irrigation system and there were always sheep to be moved, no matter what the weather.

I've always been a visitor to the countryside, nipping in for a day's fishing here and there and maybe doing a spot of hiking in the mountains. I've never really felt part of it, though, part of its pastoral rhythms and its cycles of birth and death. Rachel cried when the first lamb died, but later, when we lost 20 in a late snow, it didn't really bother her. I was much worse; after feeding Ping and Pong every day for two months, I was inconsolable when I found out that they were going to be dinner on Christmas day.

I'm trying not to be soppy here, so I will plagiarise to make my point. Barb and Stuart had a framed poem on their wall and I hope they won't mind if I quote it here. It's called The Farmer's Creed and has been traced back to a farmer named Frank Mann, who was certainly more effusive than Stuart when he penned it in 1915.

Anyway, it explains what I am trying to say far more eloquently than I ever could:

The Farmer's Creed

I believe a man's greatest possession is his dignity
and that no calling bestows this more abundantly than
farming.

I believe hard work and honest sweat are the
building blocks of a person's character.

I believe that farming, despite its hardships
and disappointments, is the most honest
and honourable way a man can spend his
days on this earth.

I believe farming nurtures the close family
ties that make life rich in ways money
can't buy.

I believe my children are learning values that
will last a lifetime and can be learned in no
other way.

I believe farming provides education for life and that
no other occupation teaches so much about birth,
growth, and maturity in such a variety of ways.

I believe many of the best things in life are indeed
free: the splendour of a sunrise, the rapture of wide
open spaces, the exhilarating sight of your land
greening each spring.

I believe that true happiness comes from watching your crops ripen in the field, your children grow tall in the sun, your whole family feel the pride that springs from their shared experience.

I believe that by my toil I am giving more to the world than I am taking from it, an honour that does not come to all men.

I believe my life will be measured ultimately by what I have done for my fellow man, and by this standard I fear no judgement.

I believe when a man grows old and sums up his days, he should be able to stand tall and feel pride in the life he's lived.

I believe in farming because it makes all this possible.

16 A RIVER OF MY OWN

Spring brings something else in New Zealand, something of special interest to feral fishermen. The first day of the fishing season. Barb and Stuart's son was home from boarding school, and as soon as work was finished, Angus and I headed down the valley to a rather well-known river 10 minutes' drive down the road. Earlier in the year, in the closed winter season, I had walked its banks looking for trout, but the levels were high and I hadn't seen a thing in the muddy swirling depths. It was a changed river now. There hadn't been much rain and the river was low, sustained by snowmelt and the odd shower.

You run out of superlatives for clean water when writing fishing prose, but trust me here – if it was a French door, your dog would have run into it. This was a lowland river flowing a fairly gentle gradient through farmland. It should have at least had a tinge to it, like the photographs in my fishing guides. We left the car and walked upstream from the bridge.

Angus was new to fly fishing and didn't have Polaroids. I soon saw a fish holding under a tree against the opposite bank and had fun playing the expert and trying to point it out to him. When I took my glasses off, it disappeared, melting into the rocks and surface shimmer. When I made a cast, it really did disappear, under the trees and out of the way of rusty fishermen.

We carried on, walking and walking, straining our eyes to look into every likely lie, but we didn't see another, which amazed me. It was early season; this was a well-known river and I thought we were being extremely careful.

It was just getting dark when we got back to the bridge. We were on the other side of the river, so we peered through the trees to see if the first fish was back at its station. We couldn't see it, so retreated to cross the river further down, a little despondently, to tell the truth. Then Angus stopped me and pointed at a large boulder in midstream. Although the light was bad, I could quite easily see the end of a log sticking out from behind it. It was too darkly coloured to be a fish and was sticking out at a weird angle. Angus wasn't convinced and I had to poke it with the end of my rod to prove my point. The 'log' didn't like that. It bolted back under the trees. Angus didn't say anything, but I sensed our relationship changed a little right then.

The next afternoon, we were back at the river. This time we brought two cars. I left Bertha at the bridge and we drove a couple of kilometres downstream and parked Stuart's truck at a friendly farmhouse. Our idea was that we would save a walk back to the car and we would be hitting water that probably didn't get a lot of pressure.

Remembering the lesson from the night before, we slowed right down. Everything that might have been a fish we watched carefully, and then made a cast anyway. None of them were, though. There was an amazing amount of likely looking holding water and after a couple of hours, we were less than halfway to the car, with no sight or smell of a trout. We hurried up and again it was getting dark as we approached the bridge where the car was parked. There was a series of runs and pools here, which just screamed fish. We fished them blind and after a couple of casts, my little yarn indicator nipped below the surface. I had a half-second of contact and then the line went slack. I didn't care; it was better than nothing, maybe I wasn't completely useless after all.

It rained hard that night and all through the next day. We left the river alone for a couple of days, but had a good evening's fishing on a nearby lake. We didn't get any of its famous land-locked salmon, but it was good to feel the pull of the small browns that we caught fairly easily in the shallows.

Angus had to go on a rugby tour and I was sorry to see him go – he was great to fish with. I taught him about knots and rise forms and some barefoot river craft, and he taught me about the trees and the birds and all the animals of the bush, most of which he liked to shoot in his spare time. He was a quiet lad, but had a wicked sense of humour, and he changed my opinion of 15-year-olds. I suppose when you start driving a £50,000 tractor at age 12, you tend to grow up quick.

It was one of those perfect evenings when I got back to the river, calm and warm with the air alive with shimmering flying things. The water had cleared after the rain, but the level was up and it retained a milky tinge that gave me a lot more confidence. I again parked by the bridge, but only walked half a kilometre down to below the series of pools. There had been another vehicle at the bridge, but it was parked on the upstream side and I assumed that they had gone that way. I still kept an eye out for the flash of a rod downstream. It is very bad form to jump ahead of another angler, especially a local, which the battered Toyota Hilux had suggested.

With the sun at a low angle and the slight discolour, it was difficult to see into the water. I fished the first pool blind, carefully making short casts from a crouched position, working the entire area, as I had found that New Zealand fish will hold in the most unlikely of places. I thought I saw a rise, but I couldn't be sure and the indicator bobbed down unmolested. I had two flies on, a shaggy weighted Hare's Ear Nymph and a size-16 Pheasant Tail Nymph tied to the shank of the nymph on two feet of mono. The idea of this rig is for the weighted nymph to get the flies down, with the smaller unweighted fly drifting naturally a bit higher in the water.

The next section we hadn't even fished the last time. It was a long shallow run between pools that flowed at a slow walk and was very exposed, with no undercut banks, overhanging trees or even boulders to offer protection to the skittish brown trout. I was going to walk through it when I saw the unmistakable porpoise of a feeding fish. It was two feet from the left bank, about 10 metres up, in very shallow water. It was feeding voraciously, rising every few seconds, with its whole back showing above the water.

I made a cast, which was too far right and then another that was bang on. The indicator didn't move and I thought I had put the fish down. No, it started rising again almost straight away. It was in such an easy position, not even a half cast away, directly upstream so that drag wasn't an issue and there were no overhanging trees or wind to interfere with my casting, which had sharpened up considerably over the past week. I had no excuse.

I took off the bigger nymph and put five more casts over it with just the Pheasant Tail, which would have been drifting just below the surface. Again, it was ignored and the fish moved a little higher up and even closer to the bank, right under a dead branch that stuck out over the river and would have snagged a cast.

I carefully retreated and took off the nymph. I couldn't for the life of me see what the fish was feeding on, I couldn't see anything drifting past my legs and there was nothing on the surface, either. Even so, I put on a Parachute Adams with a simple rust-coloured Hare and Copper on the shank. This is a great fly that has become a favourite of mine. It doesn't look like much, just a tail of hare's-ear fibres or mongoose – anything brown with a bit of movement, and a dubbed body of hare's ear ribbed with copper wire, gold wire or even black or brown thread on the smaller patterns. You tease out a few fibres so that you end up with a little brown blob that even the pickiest of trophy fish will take confidently.

The fish was still rising, but still against the bank under the branch. I crept carefully into position and put a cast as close to the end of the obstruction as I dared. In such shallow water, it was just too far out of the trout's window of view. I tried again and put it dead on, it must have missed the branch by two inches. The fish rose just as the Adams floated past and I struck, thinking that it had taken the nymph, but no. I took a few more paces and was now less than two rod-lengths away from it. I could actually see individual spots on its side when it rolled.

It was a ridiculous situation. I was standing in gently flowing water halfway up my calf – if I had a cricket bat, I could have walked up and clubbed the fish on the head. I wasn't sure if that's legal in New Zealand, though. I tried a strange sideways cast that slapped the Adams down on the water to the right of the twig, but swung the nymph around to the left and straight down the trout's alley. It floated back to my legs, so I tried it again.

This time, the leader caught on the twig, dangling the Adams just above the water with the nymph dragging on the water below. The weight of the line started pulling it, and miraculously, it dropped off without getting snagged. At that moment the fish rose again, right in front of me, under my rod. It had dropped back again and I couldn't believe it hadn't seen me. It must have drifted backwards in that lazy way that fish do.

I didn't dare move now, but I leant to my left, into the grass on the bank and flicked aggressively, as there was only three feet of fly line out the end eye. Improbably, the leader landed dead straight and gently and the bedraggled Adams floated back, its white tuft only just visible in the surface. Then it disappeared in a bulge of brown water and the fish was on. For an obvious glutton, it had a lot of energy, thrashing its tail in the shallow water as it took off upstream. I let it run, following it up to the pool above, where it stayed until I could gently net it – an elegant long fish with a wide tail and strong colour, five pounds of New Zealand's finest. It had taken the Hare and Copper, which had lodged tight in the corner of its jaw. I don't usually kill fish, but I sure enjoyed that one, cooked by Barb the following evening in her anarchic farm kitchen.

In the following weeks, I fished all the rivers in the area, but that stretch remained my favourite. It was always clearer than the others and I never ran into another angler. I never caught more than two fish an evening and I got skunked a couple of times, but I learnt so much and I got to know the water really well. I knew that what had seemed like barren water at 4pm would become alive a half hour before dark, as long dark shapes emerged from the undercut banks and deep pools to feed in the shallows. I learnt that when the water was clear and it was still light, the only chance of a fish was to spot one feeding and make a perfect cast – any drag or disturbance and it was off. When the water was discoloured, it was okay to fish blind and when it was just about dark, the best option was a big dry fly drifted down the edges of the runs.

I came to know two fish in a shallow pool that I tried night after night. They would feed in front of a boulder in midstream, returning to the cover of the trees with the slightest movement. I would crawl up in the grass to make sure they were there and then retreat to make a cast. They always held in exactly the same place and liked their food off the surface, rising to just about anything that drifted over their heads, except my flies, that is. Mayflies, caddis, beetles, even cicadas – I tried everything.

Our time on the farm was coming to end, and the last time I saw them was just before Christmas. My old friend Mark Hewat had arrived from South Africa for an extended fishing trip, and was just two hours off the plane from Christchurch when I took him down to the river at sunset for his first taste of New Zealand. He had been on planes and in airports for a day and a half and I thought the sight of two big brownies would blow the cobwebs away and get the excitement going for the rest of his trip. I think you know what is coming next.

He caught one of the fish with a beautiful long cast that couldn't have been more perfect if it had been a strand of silk floating down from heaven. I saw the whole thing. I was five feet away, on my belly in the long grass above the fish. He caught it with a single Royal Wulff that he had picked up in South Africa. He lent me another one and walking back to the car in near pitch black, I caught a belter of a trout after we thought we saw a rise in the pool under the bridge and I had a cast just in case. It was deep and muscular and looked silver in the torchlight. I still think it must have been my first New Zealand sea trout, and I couldn't have been happier as I slipped it back into the stretch of river that I now regarded as my own.

17 A SURPRISE IN SOUTHLAND

Do you know what I like about fishing? Forrest Gump said the same thing about life: "It's like a box of chocolates – you never know what you're going to get." Although I never really understood that, because if you bought a box of Cadburys Milk Tray – odds are that you will probably get a Cadburys Milk Tray – and if you're not sure what type, you just look at the little picture on the lid that tells you what shape each one is. Maybe they didn't have those pictures in the 70s. It must have been like Russian roulette for people with nut allergies.

What I mean is that unless you actually put a fly in the water, you never know what kind of day you are going to have, and what surprises lie in store for you. New Zealand is a good place for surprises. We were down the bottom of the South Island and we had been fishing hard for 10 days. Hitting the river at first light and getting back after dark for days in a row is going to take its toll. We caught some good fish, and Mark latched onto a real monster, even by New Zealand standards. It was in headwaters of the magnificent Ōreti river, and we put more than 30 casts over it between us before Mark hooked it. He had it on for 10 minutes before it snapped off under a collapsed bank – we caught a few in the six-to-eight-pound range, and this one looked twice the size.

Well, to tell the truth, we were a little jaded. Our nerves were ragged and I kept on catching Mark staring into space with a dreamy look and the hint of a tear in the corner of his eye. So we decided to take a day off from fishing and meet up with Rachel and a friend who had been on a big hiking trip in the fjords and were on the way to do all the crazy adrenaline stuff that you can do around Queenstown. They were passing through that day and we arranged to meet for lunch in nearby Te Anau.

It was a gorgeous day when we woke; clear skies and hardly a breeze ruffling the pine trees – a rare occurrence in Southland at any time of the year. We hung around the lodge a bit, had a big breakfast and wondered what we could do to kill a few hours. So we decided to go fishing. Now you might think that going fishing is a strange thing to do on a day off from fishing. But you see, we weren't going fishing properly. Let me explain.

A couple of days before, we had crossed a little stream on our way to a well-known trophy river and we had stopped on the bridge to have a look, because that's what you do when you've got lots of time on your hands and you've fished three of the world's most famous rivers in the past week. If a stream is smaller than a river, then this was a streamlet. It was just perfect, though; clear as a wine glass and trickling over white stones in a sheltered pastoral valley. Just the kind of river for a day off. We worked out what it was called from the map, but could only find a fleeting reference to it in one of our fishing guides, an older book that said something like "a charming small stream that should be fished with the dry-fly."

Now I could write a whole book on reading between the lines in New Zealand fishing guides. Let me give you an example:

"A challenging trophy river" – prepare for disappointment – you might see some fish as big as your leg, but it will be as they shoot off for cover and you will spend the whole day feeling like your expensive five-weight rod has got all the finesse of a barge pole.

"A popular river with a good head of lively fish" – it's where the local kids go to fish with worms and catch palm-sized tiddlers by the dozen. A good option for restoring confidence after a day on "a challenging trophy river".

"A lively river with hard-fighting residents" – the river will look something like the Zambezi below Victoria Falls. Inflatable rafts full of adrenalin-junkie backpackers will come sweeping past you all day. The fish are hard-fighting because they have to be supremely fit to

avoid ending up in the sea. Don't wear waders. Make sure your will is up to date.

"A river made famous by Zane Grey" – absolutely chock-full of visiting American anglers, each with kit worth more than the GDP of Lesotho. Avoid at all costs.

"An interesting river that will reward the fit angler" – at last, something positive. Remember that the aforementioned VAAs keep the helicopter guides in business and are not that keen on physical exertion. The locals are hardier, but will know five other rivers in the area that aren't in the guidebook and that they can access with ease through their brother-in-law's farm.

So, what do we make of "a charming small stream that should be fished with the dry-fly"? It's a difficult one, really. The fact that it wasn't in any of the new-edition guidebooks might suggest that it isn't as good as it was. But then again, rivers go up and down from season to season, depending on local rainfall, rod pressure, and even local farming practice. The use of the word 'charming' suggests a certain Lilliputian attraction, and the advice to fish with the dry fly tells me that it is an easy river which would be unsporting to fish with the nymph. Basically, I was expecting a pretty piece of water that might be barren, but might have a few smallish residents that we could catch fairly easily on the dry fly. Just the thing for a day off from 'proper' New Zealand fishing.

We found a farm track that led upstream from the bridge and managed to get a fair distance away from the road before we parked in a grove of trees. We tackled up leisurely, with none of the four-thumbed fumbling that we had been prone to lately. I hadn't even bought my wading boots and just had a trusty pair of wellies. The first section was just lovely, a small waterfall spilled into a long pool that curved under an undercut bank on the far side. It looked perfect.

To prove how relaxed I was, there was no customary game of rock-paper-scissors to see who got the first cast. I offered to cross lower down and spot for Mark from above the undercut. The water seeped over my wellies at the tail of the pool and I was complaining loudly when I crawled through the grass on the bank to peer over the edge. Bloody hell! A six-pound rainbow! Right below me, not four feet from my nose, feeding avidly with a slightly smaller one behind. So much for a "charming bloody small stream", this was serious.

It was a difficult cast – and anyway, the fish were probably a bit spooked with me stomping around above their heads. We moved on upstream, leapfrog-fishing the pools, as the runs were just too shallow and exposed. I soon saw a classic rise in a shallow pool. I covered it with a Parachute Adams with a little bead head nymph as a dropper.

The fish smacked the Adams right away and took off downstream, straight past me, its broad back sticking half out the water in the shallow riffle. It was a good fish but I played it hard, worried that it would damage itself on the rocks. Mark took some pictures as I managed to get below it and try for an early netting, so I am happy to report that Mark has a lovely sequence of me demonstrating how not to net a fish. I came at it from below, it shot through my legs and I stood on my leader, snapping it in an instant. At least Mark was laughing again after his 'Ōreti, biggest fish of a lifetime lost' incident. I didn't swear nearly as much, though.

We then came to a section that wrapped along the edge of a collapsed bank, which had brought down several big pine trees. They lay across the stream like pick-up-sticks for giants, creating 20 perfect lies that were impossible to get at. I had a go anyway and got snagged up on my first cast. Me climbing over trees to retrieve my fly also seemed amusing to Dr Hewat, as he got out the camera to capture more of my incompetence for posterity. As I was reaching over to get my fly, a long shape bolted out of the shadow below me, followed by another and then another further up. These were also big fish, but I was thrilled rather than annoyed. It was my day off, after all.

The next section was deep in the forest, a long slow pool that was surprisingly deep and mysterious, one of those places that look like they should be sheltering the fish of lifetime, or a crocodile, but is usually as barren as Ermelo on a Sunday morning. I took the dry fly off and put on a single big Hares-Ear Nymph with a little strike indicator about ten feet up the leader. Casting space was limited, but I managed a sort of flick up against the opposite bank – the kind of cast that you could only pull off after 10 straight days of fishing. Ask me to do it now and it would take me 20 attempts to get it right.

The indicator washed up tight against the opposite back. Swirling gently against the roots of a drowned tree, it suddenly disappeared below the surface. Thinking that the fly had snagged, I lifted the rod carefully. The rainbow attached to the other end bucked deep under the undercut back and I stumbled back trying to take up the slack. After a strong fight up and down the length of the pool, I beached it and was surprised that it was only about four pounds.

Still fishless, Mark headed off downstream to some promising-looking water below the car. We only had about half an hour left before we had to head back and I had a bit more of a poke around in the pools, but it was impossible to spot fish in the shade of the trees and I only succeeded in spooking another big fish at the tail of a pool, that I only saw when I was about to stand on it. The movement of my hand unclipping the fly from its clasp was enough to send it scooting upstream.

I headed back to look for Mark and was surprised that we had only covered about 400m from the car – usually in New Zealand, you walk kilometres during the day to make casts to a handful of sighted fish. This was one populous river!

He was well camouflaged in the spring grass, and if it wasn't for the flash of sunlight off his rod, I would have missed him completely. The sun was flashing off his rod because it was doing the sickle-shaped fish dance and Mark was holding on for dear life as a good trout tried to get back under the bank that it had just left to suck in his little nymph. It wasn't a double-figure beast like his friend from the Ōreti, but it looked out of place in the picture-postcard little run that didn't even spill over my boots. Mark landed it gently and released it almost lovingly. With another few weeks of fishing together ahead, I could have kissed that fish for putting the flick back in my friend's cast.

We really had to go then and as we packed our gear and floored it back to Te Anau, we talked of what a magical, surprising morning it had been. I can't remember a two-hour stretch of fishing that has given me more pleasure. Even though the famous Mataura gave me my biggest fish ever, and the Río Gallegos in Patagonia showered fish on me like some divine plague, my favourite river in the world is a tiny, little-known stream in a quiet corner of New Zealand. And you will excuse me if I don't say exactly which corner that is.

18 MARK HEWAT BITES THE BEAR

I complain about them, but I actually really like Americans. I'm usually just jealous that the ones I meet seem to have much more disposable income than I do! They are generally very friendly, enthusiastic, and can be extremely entertaining, whether they mean to be or not.

I guess the folk that vote in the wholly unqualified right-wing presidents probably don't have passports, as the yanks I've met while travelling have all been lovely and roll their eyes when you mention their incumbent leader. We ran into a classic example early on in our trip at a backcountry campsite in the Marlborough region of the South Island. He was my kind of guy, in a heterosexual, macho kind of way, of course. He had been in the country for two months and had a plastic bag full of topographical maps that he was using to hike his way across the country, fishing the best bits as he went along. And get this – he had caught seven trout over 10 pounds, including two that day! We were agog, we had blanked that day, this guy was an absolute legend! He just shrugged and said with a laconic drawl, "Some days you bite the bear, some days the bear bites you."

I kept that bit of philosophy with me. It has helped me through some difficult times, times when doubts have crept in, when I began to wonder what an educated, otherwise sane individual was doing up to his waist in some frigid river, not catching anything and then not catching anything and breaking his expensive fly rod, for the second time that year.

No matter how much you love fly fishing, and I love it as much as anyone, there are going to be days when you just don't enjoy it – the bear days. The days when you wonder what you would be doing at that instant if, all those years ago, you had picked up an accountancy textbook and said, 'this is going to be my passion'.

The thing about bears is that they don't like company. They are loners. When that bear takes a bite out of you, he is satiated, he is going to ignore your buddy on the next run up. He might even get careless and turn his back for a minute, allowing your lucky friend to creep up and bite him squarely on his furry rear. Let me tell you about such a day; the day Mark Hewat bit the bear.

We were up north again, still on the South Island, but we had left the jagged peaks of the Southern Alps for the lesser-known region around the settlement of Hanmer Springs. I don't know what it is, but international anglers don't seem that keen on this area. It might be the aesthetics – it isn't quite as pretty as Queenstown or Nelson Province – but there are fewer sand flies and the trout are just as pretty and just as big.

There is a tonne of water in the area, but most of it can only be reached by helicopter or by hiking a very long way, which is difficult because there is no right to roam in New Zealand and you have to know exactly where you are going. It helps immensely if the owner of the lodge that you are staying at is also a helicopter pilot with the local guiding service and likes the irony of showing his guests how to walk into water that the fly-in clients pay thousands of dollars to be dropped off at.

There are some big rivers in the area, big enough that there is a jetboat operation that scares the crap out of backpackers for £50 a go. When levels are low, you can walk the banks and spot some very large trout on the edges of the pools. Levels are hardly ever low, so I guess they go unmolested for most of the year. There is loads of water like this in New Zealand, large rivers that are very seldom fished because of their size, and because the fish move up and down them depending on conditions. They hold some incredible specimens, though. We saw the carcass of a 26lb rainbow that had been caught that morning by a spin fisherman and was being stored in the bait fridge at the local hardware store, because no other fridge could fit it. That puts things in perspective a bit.

The day before, we had fished the Clarence River. It's a medium-sized river and flows in a remote featureless valley that entails a rather exciting drive up a steep switchback behind Hanmer Springs and then down into the next valley. That is when things started going wrong for me.

It was a windy day and, with that 26lb monster in the back of my mind, I decided to fish a sinking line with a very large weighted Woolly Bugger that I was planning to rip through the deep pools in the hope of tempting something similar. To tell the truth, I was just being lazy. Mark stuck with a double nymph rig and a big indicator and headed off upstream. I was really pumping the cast in the wind, throwing across to the opposite bank so that the line would sink nice and deep into the pool. I was fishing my favourite rod, a nine-foot Orvis with a very fast action. I had hated it when I first got it but after a few weeks, I think it taught me to cast properly. All of a sudden, I could be casting a size-six Muddler Minnow in the wind one day and then throwing a short line with a dry fly to a sighted fish.

You can imagine how annoyed I was when there was that awful splintering noise as I cast, as the pieces become unstuck and broke against each other. It's the third time that has happened to me. Why don't I ever learn to check the join every now and again? My spare rod was back at the lodge, so I helped myself to Mark's from the back of the car. It was a six weight and much heavier than I was used to. I felt like Lewis Hamilton would if his Ferrari broke down and the courtesy car from the garage was a Vauxhall Cavalier.

I stuck with the sinker and headed off upstream to find Mark. It was a desolate, treeless valley and I could see him from a long way off. You know how you can tell from a person's posture that there is something going on? Well, Mark looked like my cat does when she's stalking a bird in the garden – all hunched concentration. He was fishing the eye of a pool where the flow dissipated into deeper water. Even as I approached him, he struck as the yarn indicator was snatched under the surface. The fish stayed on for a couple of seconds before spitting the fly. It was about his fifth take in the pool; he had landed one fish and had lost another, which he had estimated at about eight pounds when it jumped.

I persuaded him to give the pool a break and carry on up with me. We walked and fished for a couple of hours, with our only success being a tiny rainbow that was not much bigger than the fly that it ate.

We eventually came to a long deep pool that looked a lot more promising. I crossed at the tail end, slipping on the rocks and almost falling on my rod... well, Mark's rod. We started working our way up and within a minute, Mark let out a yell and was into a proper fish. It broke the surface immediately and we could see right away that it was solid. To avoid incident, I put down the rod and crossed back onto Mark's side to lend a hand and take some photos.

The fish was really giving Mark a workout, running up and down the pool and not letting him recover any line. It then headed downstream and Mark put on all the pressure that he dared to stop it going down the impressive rapid below. He could do nothing and we had to scramble over the rocks in pursuit. This was an unbelievably strong fish and it just didn't seem to tire. This went on for ages – every time we got to a bit of slack water, Mark would do everything he could to subdue the fish, but time and time again, it just headed downstream. It eventually rolled on its side in a shallow riffle and we realised why – it was hooked firmly through the back. Mark was disappointed, but at least he didn't have to walk 20 minutes upstream to find the fishing rod that he had put down, with the metaphorical bear following all the way.

That night, we had a few beers with the lodge owner. After hearing the sorry story of our day, and perhaps because we had bought the beers, he took pity on us and drew us a map on the back of the beer carton. He said that it would lead us to a tributary that the guiding service used when the weather was rough and windy, that we should be prepared for some very large fish and we should keep it to ourselves, on pain of death.

With a lot of driving and walking ahead of us, we made an early start with our precious piece of cardboard. The sun had yet to rise and a thick morning mist slowed us down as we looked for the turnoff that we needed. We drove up a certain remote road, into a remote valley, took a rough side track for a while, parked our car out of view in a dip and headed cross country until we reached a large river. We swam across it as instructed and headed downstream until we found a small tributary that entered the main river in a steep gorge.

From the top of the cliffs the tributary looked tiny and not worth investigating, but as we followed it upstream, we realised that it was quite a bit bigger than we had first thought. While it was narrow, it was also very deep and in the open sections, it was the same size as the streams in Southland where we had sight fished (mostly unsuccessfully) to double-digit browns. The quivers of excitement started in our bellies.

The mist had cleared by now and the strengthening sun dried our clothes as we looked for the point that the lodge owner had told us to start fishing. We never got there. Bypassing a gorge section littered with enormous boulders, I caught the unmistakable silhouette of a large fish feeding avidly in a side eddy below. Mark won the rock-paper-scissors and I lost sight of him as he crept off between the boulders to get into position. I got on my belly and edged my way to the edge of the cliff above the pool, something I seemed to have been doing a lot of lately.

I couldn't resist taking a couple of photos and could plainly see that the fish was taking a hatch of pale caddis-like insects off the surface. Mark had decided to try a size-16 Parachute Adams with a tiny bead-head nymph on the dropper and it looked like a wise decision.

After several minutes, I still couldn't see him and was starting to get a little frustrated. It didn't help when I spotted another torpedo shape a little higher up the pool, and then another that was even bigger and an unusual greenish colour. Three browns of this size in the same pool is the kind of scenario that I had only ever read about, and I am sorry that you have to do the same.

Mark eventually appeared way downstream, clambering along the steep edge of the gorge. He got as far as he could without falling in, but it was still a long and difficult cast, the current was going to cause all sorts of drag problems and he couldn't see his target. He was going to have to trust me to guide his cast. The first three attempts were off-target, too short, too short and left and then way left. With growing irritation, I let Mark know what I thought of his casting.

The fourth cast was in the right postcode, but the timing was off and the flies and leader landed in a heap just behind the fish. This was a blessing in disguise. In the second that it took for the current to straighten the line, the fish must have caught a movement in the corner of its eye. It whipped around and rushed the yard or so to where the Adams was getting swirled around in a little eddy. It sucked it in confidently and I screamed, "Strike, strike, strike!" Mark was as surprised as I was but lifted his rod and the hook stuck.

Forgetting the other browns for an instant, I jumped to my feet in excitement and did a celebratory jig. The only place we could net the fish was downstream, and miraculously it headed that way of its own accord. We were able to net it a few minutes later in a quiet corner. About six to seven pounds in weight, it was healthy and solid and recovered quickly after a brief photo session.

It was now my turn. We returned to my position on the cliff and after a couple of minutes, saw one of the other fish. It had moved a little higher into the eye of the pool and was still feeding avidly, we could see a flash of white every few seconds as it opened its mouth to take a hatching insect sub-surface. I slid down the rock face below us and was able to get a lot closer than Mark had, although I had to cast over a flat rock in midstream which obscured my view completely. On the second cast, Mark yelled "Now! Strike! It's on!" Of course, by that time it wasn't and must have been pricked as it bolted for the cover of deeper water. Mark said that it grabbed the little bead head straight away and mouthed it for a second before spitting it out.

We retired to the shade to calm our nerves and give the pool a chance to settle. Unbelievably, when we returned to our vantage point, we saw the green fish straight away. It was holding in the exact place that my pricked fish had just vacated. What happened next was almost inevitable. Mark hooked it on the first cast and landed it after an interesting battle that saw him swimming down the gorge as the fish ran. Its back was indeed a deep green, and it was a magnificently healthy specimen. I managed one blurred photo before the camera battery died and silently resigned myself to the role of official fish spotter for the day.

We kept walking, always on the lookout for fish and blind fishing likely sections with no result. Then, on the edge of a long rapid, we saw a real monster of a trout feeding in full view, only a foot or two from the bank. 14, 15, 16 pounds? I don't know, but it was the biggest fish I have ever seen.

We had been taking turns and you guessed it, it was Mark's turn. He made one perfect cast, the fish turned to follow the Adams as it bobbed down the run and then disappeared into the tumult as soon as drag set in. Sad story and all, but don't feel too bad, Mark made a few blind casts into the area and moments later, hooked another boring six pounder that was as strong and wilful as the others. He eventually eased it to the shallows for me to net, something I was getting quite proficient at.

Fishing blind, the rough section gave us a few more small fish and even the official spotter managed a couple. Having not brought any food and with one of us nursing a throbbing wrist, we called it a day and headed back to the car. Swimming the large river in the afternoon heat was a lot more pleasant and we were truly elated with the day's fishing.

You hear all sort of stories from the world's fishing hotspots, but consider this – this was Mark's first trip to New Zealand, we didn't have a guide, we are intermediate fishermen at best and before this trip, his biggest river fish was under two pounds. Three brown trout between six and eight pounds in a couple of hours – including two sight fished on a tiny dry. It doesn't get much better than that. Mark dined on bear that day.

I'd like to end the story there, but I'm afraid that our day was far from over. We were still buzzing as we packed up the car. Our mood only changed when I tried to start it. The battery was flat as a pancake. I had forgotten to switch off the headlights when we arrived in the mist that morning. I had parked in a depression off to the side of the track, which was the worst possible place for a push start. We tried anyway, but only succeeded in pushing Bertha into a ditch. Reality began to dawn. We hadn't seen another person all day, we were about 30 kilometres from the public road and it would be dark in an hour.

We had a think about our options. It was midsummer and 30 kilometres is a manageable walk, but the temperature can plummet at night in the mountains and it can snow at any time of the year. Our clothes were still damp from the swim and it just wasn't worth risking the walk in the dark when we could have an acceptably uncomfortable night in the car and set off at sunrise.

In our excitement that morning, we hadn't packed anything that wasn't fishing related. Anything that was in the car was there because we had been too lazy to unpack it. I had a root around and found a dry, but slightly rank pair of long johns, our tiny dome tent and a topo map under the seat that I thought we had lost a few days before. We also realised that Bertha's position in the ditch wasn't going to provide a very horizontal sleeping position and there was every chance that we would both end up in a heap in the footwell.

Looking at the map, we found more or less where we were. We were hoping for a nearby farmhouse, but it didn't look good, the only feature other than contour lines and rivers was a little icon that represented a 'Historical Place Of Interest'. We had no idea what that might be, but hoped it might be some kind of monument that we could pitch the tent behind. It was a kilometre or so up the track, so we packed up the tent and the mouldy long johns and set off into the dusk.

We almost walked straight past it. It was a little mud building; just two rooms, and unfurnished, but it had a roof, a door that closed and an information board outside saying that it was once used by early stock men to shelter from the worst of the weather. We were still a bit nervous about the plummeting temperatures, so we did what any normal person would do: we pitched the tent in the front room.

I wouldn't say that it was the most comfortable night of my life, but we didn't freeze to death, which is something that I always appreciate when camping. Brokeback Mountain jokes aside, I think our combined body heat in the little tent made all the difference.

Very early the next morning, just as the grey of dawn was taking over from the perfect black of the high-country night, I was woken by a faint rumbling noise that wasn't Mark's stomach. In my half-asleep state, I thought it was thunder, but it got closer and louder and I recognised the unmistakable rumble of a diesel engine. I shook Mark, ripped open the tent and burst out of the hut just as a beaten old flatbed truck was approaching along the track. I jumped into its path.

I wish I could describe the driver's face. I was half asleep, I was wearing stained Long Johns, and I was rambling incoherently about fishing, car lights and jump leads. He looked at me, there was a moment of amazed silence, and then he said in a strong Eastern European accent, "I've got hives." Well that is what he meant to say; with his Slavic twang it sounded more like, "I've got ggg'ives."

I stared at him blankly for a second; it actually crossed my mind that I might still be asleep. He must have seen the confusion on my face and gestured to the back of the truck where I now noticed several wooden beehives lashed together. He explained that he had to go drop the hives off at various locations up the valley and that he would be back to pick us up in two to three hours. He didn't have jump leads, but had lots of rope and it wouldn't be a problem to pull Bertha out of the ditch and tow her up the road to a flat stretch where we could push start her.

I've never been so happy to meet someone with hives. We were back in Hanmer Springs by midday and spoiled ourselves with the biggest fried breakfast you ever saw. The lodge owner had noticed that we hadn't come home, but had assumed that we couldn't drag ourselves away from the fishing and had camped out. When we checked out of the lodge a couple of days later, he actually tried to knock off the price of the night that we hadn't slept in our beds. We wouldn't hear any of it, especially Mark, who was still grinning like a lottery winner and threatening to hug the poor guy.

19 A NEW ZEALAND HANGOVER

Hanmer Springs is fairly remote, but we moved onto somewhere that isn't even named on the map. We chanced on a dilapidated old farm store that advertised rooms to rent. It was run by a barmy Polish lady who subsidised her income by making various products out of the possums that one of her permanent lodgers shot for her. The lodger was also an interesting chap, prone to walking around the grounds with his shotgun, wearing nothing but Y-fronts and boots.

It's amazing what you can make out of possum fur. Our hostess took a bit of a shine to me and asked me coquettishly one evening:

"So Davey, vould you like to see my furry neeple caps?"

She showed them to us, along with her possum-fur knickers and range of willy warmers. Rural New Zealand can be a funny place.

Poor Mark wasn't laughing. His luck had run out, blanking for three days in a row, getting savaged by sand flies and then dropping the end section of his favourite rod into Lake Rotoiti. Lake Rotoiti is quite deep. It was his last week and perhaps he started to fall into the trap of rushing to cram as much fishing as possible into each day. I fared a bit better, but then I had three more months ahead of me and maybe the fish sensed that I wasn't as desperate to catch them.

When Rachel and I took off from Auckland airport in late April on our way to Bali, I had no regrets. Every box was ticked in thick black marker pen. I love New Zealand and I will go back there one day. The thing is, there are so many other wild and alluring places to chase trout that I have yet to visit. I've never been to North America, Russia has always appealed… and I still had to give myself the chance of catching a wild salmon. Plans had already started hatching in my head.

But then a funny thing happened when I got back to the UK after two months in the tropics. Where we live in South West England, we are surrounded by some fantastic waters by most peoples' standards. The picturesque large reservoirs near our home produce naturally grown on trout up to 20 pounds, and pike over 40lbs. Just about every river and stream in the county holds wild browns and sea trout and it is a cheap flight across to the legendary fisheries of Ireland or up to the Scottish Highlands.

But I'd lost my taste for it. It wasn't the same. As I have since I was a child, I thought about fishing all the time. But I wasn't daydreaming about English reservoirs, or famous Scottish rivers. In my mind, I was back in the South Island high country, following a nameless tributary, casting small flies to huge, sighted fish in crystal water. Nothing else could compare.

The weeks turned into months and the months into a year. With the internal itch completely gone, we bought a nice house in the country, Rachel and I finally got married and we had our first baby. Unbelievably, it was two years before I cast a line again. I've got my new daughter to thank. She was delivered by caesarean and Rach had to spend a few days in hospital recovering, with me keeping her company in the chair at the bottom of her bed. The newsagent in the hospital sold a wide range of magazines, including a couple of fishing ones. At first, I managed to ignore them. I read Time, Newsweek and GQ. It was finally a choice between Hello and Trout And Salmon. I relented. With my tiny new daughter asleep on my chest, I read it cover to cover in a couple of hours. I read about new buzzer patterns, new tying materials and how the mild winters of the past few years had actually been good for the fishing, with trout maintaining their condition like never before.

Three weeks later, and only after I had met my weekly nappy quota, I was up to my thighs in a quiet inlet of a lake near my home. I fished a team of freshly tied buzzers under a yarn indicator. It was a beautiful spring afternoon, the countryside was starting to stir after another mild winter and with every cast, I eased further into a familiar peace that was like the final piece of the jigsaw slipping into place. It didn't matter too much, but I eventually hooked a small rainbow just before dark. More importantly, it was me that was hooked again. The New Zealand hangover was finally gone.

20 YOBS WITH BLOBS

South Africans in the UK have got a reputation for working hard and playing harder. They are also known for being a little on the blunt side and calling a spade a spade. In the workplace this can actually be quite useful as you get to bypass the niceties of the UK class system and 'get shit done', as my old boss used to say. Finally, we have a reputation for being extremely competitive. Apart from the hard-working bit, I admit that I am guilty on all other counts.

Fishing a remote river on your own, if you blank you just tell yourself that there were no fish in that section of river and move on. But on a lake with a few other anglers, if you blank while everyone else is catching, then that really tickles that competitive Saffa gene.

I'm no expert, but I liked to think that I wasn't completely useless after 25 years chasing trout. I did okay on the little streams and rivers where my standard upstream nymph tactics seemed acceptable to the wild browns and stocked rainbows. The big lakes were a different story, though. I couldn't seem to catch a cold.

I fluked the occasional fish, but on numerous occasions I blanked while locals on either side of me caught fish after fish, bopping them on the head until they reached their eight-fish limit when they would pack up and leave, no doubt to sell them for £5 a pop. I would surreptitiously slip into their recently vacated spot where I assumed the fish were shoaled up, but would be lucky to catch just one, even though I thought that I was fishing the same method with the same sorts of flies.

I started getting a bit obsessive. I spent a lot of time watching YouTube videos on big reservoir tactics, I read every magazine article on the subject that I could find and I started interrogating any anglers that

I came across that seemed to have the secret key that I lacked.

I've no doubt that I scared a couple with my zeal, but one of them helpfully suggested that I join the local fishing club. The Bristol Reservoirs Fly Fishing Association, to give it its full title, holds fly-tying evenings, social events, and runs regular competitions on the lakes during the summer. Competition fishing was new to me, but it is hugely popular in the UK, with my local lakes being venues for club, national and even international competitions. Newbies like me are paired with experienced anglers, and it turned out that some of those local fish mongers had fished for England, and one had even captained the team in the World Championship. I didn't feel quite as bad about getting outfished, and concentrated on soaking up as much information as I could.

I had gradually got used to casting a team of three or four flies without getting too many tangles, but I didn't give much thought to what flies I used and didn't appreciate that a team of flies should be selected to work together to improve the overall success. You know, like a team.

There are all sorts of combinations that work well for different reasons, but some of them are blindingly obvious when you think about it. A bright and gaudy Blob fly made from synthetic fritz may not look like anything natural, but it certainly stands out and attracts the inquisitive trout in for a closer look. This is hugely important on a big deep lake where the fish can be spread out over a vast area. If you team it with a couple of more natural nymphs, then the trout will often come in to investigate the Blob and then take one of the nymphs behind it. To be honest they just as often take the Blob, so it can be a very effective approach.

I also learnt that at times, trout will feed exclusively at a particular level for one reason or another. One major benefit of a team of flies is that it allows you to cover a wide range of depths until you find where the fish are feeding. Realising this was my biggest eureka moment, and probably saved me from giving up on the lakes altogether and taking up golf.

With a floating line, if you put a heavy fly on the point and two lighter flies at five-foot intervals up the leader, then you can fish three significantly different depths. If you just cast out three light flies and retrieved, then all the flies would be no more than three or four feet down and you could be completely missing a feeding frenzy taking place a few more feet down. How much time did I waste fishing layers of water that were barren of fish?

Once you find the right level, then you can adapt your setup so that you can put all your flies in the 'killing zone' for as long as possible. You can achieve this by switching to an intermediate or sinking line, using neutral-density flies, or just leaving your flies static so they hang naturally or sink very slowly. Even swapping monofilament for slightly heavier fluorocarbon tippet can make a difference.

On other occasions, the fish can be incredibly picky and fixate on one type of insect, or a very specific size and colour. One size too big, or the wrong shade of green and you can't catch a thing. Trickier still is when fish become obsessed with a particular stage of the hatching process. There could be thousands of buzzer pupa rising from the lake bed to hatch at the surface, but the fish could only be taking them at the exact moment that they burst from their pupal shuck in the surface film before flying away. Everything else is ignored and it can drive a person insane with frustration. Traditional dry flies that sit on top of the water just don't work – what you really need on these occasions is an emerger.

The real gamechanger for me was sharing a boat with a guy called Martin who has a reputation for being a bit of a guru at this tactic. His pattern of choice is a simple emerger called a Bob's Bits. It is literally just a slim body of seal's fur and then a sparse hackle in a matching colour. You rough up the fur on a bit of Velcro, apply a bit of floatant and end up with a chaotic little jumble of fibres that sits right in the surface film – just like a hatching insect that is all legs and shuck and new wings.

The eponymous Bob apparently pulled a few strands from his woolly jumper to make the prototype fly, but it is generally accepted that seal's fur is the best option for the dubbing, with red, claret and rusty brown being the most productive colours on my local waters.

Of course, Martin's success was down to more than the flies he used. What made him a true master was his almost supernatural ability to spot trout and then place a fly a foot ahead of them where they could easily see it. Fish swimming just under the surface have a tiny field of vision and with my inability to see them, I could only lob out my flies blindly and hope that a fish would happen upon them. I fluked a couple, but in three hours, Martin managed 14 without really trying that hard. He was mostly chatting, pouring us a few red wines, and taking phone calls from others on the lake who could no doubt see his rod bending and were wondering what his secret was. He opened up a whole new facet of the sport to me that I have practising ever since, just like a proper purist.

As my knowledge grew, my catches gradually improved and amazingly, I even won one of the club competitions on a windy wet day when I found a pod of fish feeding on the bottom in the middle of Heron's Bay. One of them was an old battler of five pounds that was covered in healed scars from an encounter with a big pike. When I cleaned it later, I found a partially decomposed perch in its stomach. It just shows, there is always a bigger fish in the pond.

I fished a few more competitions, but after a while I lost my taste for it. I once read a quote from a well-known angling writer who had become disillusioned with the competition scene and dismissed it as 'a bunch of yobs with Blobs'. I was beginning to see his point – some people just took it way too seriously, which is quite something coming from a South African. On one occasion, I shared a boat with a chap who has a reputation for being a bit of a grump. He didn't have the best day, persisting with stripping Boobies through the depths because it had worked well the day before when he was out practising. Everyone else was catching on floating lines and small nymphs left completely static, but he refused to switch. He got grumpier and grumpier and ended up ruining my day. I did at least experience a moment of pure joy that evening at the prizegiving, when I placed well above him.

On another occasion I was a paired with a jovial chap on a blustery May afternoon. He took the engine and made a course for the east shore where he assured me there were loads of fish. The problem was that with a brisk Westerly blowing, it got progressively choppier as we approached the mark at the head of Spring Bay. This didn't bother Captain Ahab one bit. He skilfully set up the drift, despite the boat rocking violently in the waves, and then proceeded to athletically cast out a team of three Blobs on a sinking line and pull them back through the tumult as fast as he could. This approach was very successful, but certainly didn't add to the stability of the vessel. He was having a whale of a time, boating fish after fish, and keeping up an animated running commentary. I was not so cheerful, feeling progressively more seasick, and only managing a solitary fish on my floating line. After four hours in the victory at sea conditions, I have never been so relieved to head back to the boat dock for the weigh-in.

The straw that broke the camel's back was fishing one of the prestigious sponsored competitions on a hot still day, conditions which really seem to put the fish off. I was paired with another of the experienced rods who was very keen to get into the prizes. As expected, it was slow going and neither of us had had a touch by midday. I was thrilled to finally get a solid pull that felt like a very good fish. It throbbed away on the end of my line and I just couldn't get it in, to the growing irritation of my boat partner who started huffing loudly and passing snarky comments about the strength of my wrist.

After 20 minutes, I eventually levered it up to the surface where we could plainly see that it was a very large pike. Over 20 pounds, probably. It was starting to tire, but the guy suggested in no uncertain terms that I snap it off to end the fight, leaving the fly in the pike's jaws. A quick jerk did the trick and the huge fish wallowed on the surface for a second before returning to the depths with a waft of a tail that was as wide as a spade. I was gutted.

That was the last competition I fished, but they have definitely given me the tools to be more successful and have introduced me to a host of good people that I can call on to share a relaxing day in a boat, without the need for Valium.

Mark was the first to take me out and show me how to handle a boat. With his shaved head and boxer's physique, he looks like he should be chucking people out of nightclubs, but he is a gentle giant and a very talented fisherman. He is also a master fly tier and I have become very accomplished at raiding his fly box when he is looking the other way. Very brave of me, given that he could probably throw me overboard with one arm.

Doug's acerbic wit is his most potent weapon, and he is not shy to use it. He has an encyclopaedic knowledge of all things fly fishing and loves his traditional loch-style techniques. He was the one who taught me the noble art of dibbling. This is a tricky but highly effective method where at the end of your retrieve, you 'dibble' the top dropper along the surface for a few feet before recasting, just like a newly hatched insect taking flight for the first time. It can often result in a fish lunging out of the depths to take the fly right under your rod tip. Heart-stopping stuff.

And finally, there is my friend Alan, who was one of the first to offer me advice and let me in on a few of the local secrets. Now retired from a career in the trade unions, he has fished the lakes for over 40 years and is one of the keenest and most enthusiastic anglers that I have ever met. We don't take it too seriously, but we definitely fish hard. A day out with Alan means that we will be fishing from dawn to dusk, with perhaps a short break for bacon butties. Just the way I like it.

Every year in late spring, we share a boat on Chew in an annual ritual that we have come to call our Lump Hunt. By early May, the water temperature is usually ideal and after a couple of months of peak buzzer hatches, the fish are in their best condition of the year. The plan is that we go in search of the bigger resident specimens in quiet corners of the lake that don't see much fishing pressure. This approach is usually spectacularly ineffective, and we soon make our way back to the usual hotspots to chase the recently stocked trout. The thing is that there are often resident fish shoaling up with the stockies, and every year Alan catches the biggest of the day. He just seems to be one of those people that exerts some weird magnetism to large trout. I just can't figure it out. On Chew Valley Lake, which is our favourite, he has probably caught 20 fish bigger than my biggest since I have known him. If I have a really good day and catch 10 fish and Alan catches five, his haul will always include the biggest of the day, without fail. Considering my competitive nature, I'm surprised we are still friends!

I've also got Alan to thank for introducing me to the world of predator fishing. I've always been interested in trout, and more lately salmon, and had written off all other species as inferior. Ridiculous snobbery when you think that rainbow trout originate from North America and are just stocked interlopers everywhere else. The local lakes hold all sorts of native species including pike, perch, roach, tench, eels and probably a few others that keep a lower profile. The pike and perch will readily take a fly, especially in the autumn when they are packing on the calories before winter.

If you are targeting trout, pike are a bit of a pain with their very sharp teeth that can easily slice through 10-pound leader material. You can use a wire trace to mitigate this, but then you worry that might put off that wily big brown trout, so you just accept that you will lose a few flies to old Esox Lucius during the day.

Perch are another matter, though. They are also a predator, but they don't have a mouth full of razor blades and don't grow quite as big. I think the UK record is about six pounds, but what they lack in size they make up for in attitude with their bold black stripes, red fins and 'if it moves I will try and eat it' approach to feeding.

At first, I saw them as a pest fish. I only wanted to catch big trout and it was annoying when these two- and three-pound perch kept grabbing my big streamer flies at the end of the season. Alan loves them though, and I gradually came around to their charms.

What really shifted my perception of the plucky perch was a few winter sessions purposely trying to catch them on my local river. I could catch the tiddlers quite easily on spinners or worm, but the larger ones were infuriatingly picky. I eventually caught one of about a pound, which felt like a major victory.

Now a three-pound perch on fly is an absolute prize and I really look forward to our Autumn sessions on Chew when the predators smash into the shoals of fry that congregate around the boat dock and any other structure in the lake. There you will find us, a couple of guys with 80 years of fishing experience between us, giggling like schoolboys and egging each other on as all around us fish slash and swirl, ripping through the fry just like their pelagic ocean cousins. It is just so much fun.

So for me, fishing was never meant to be competitive. While I will gladly crush any opponent at table tennis, and sulk for days when the Boks lose, when it comes to fishing I am only really competing with myself. I fish for the challenge, the camaraderie and the fun, not to catch a tonne of trout – although on the rare occasions that it happens, that is rather fun, too.

21 SEVEN YEARS IN THE SALMON DESERT

I had been a trout fisherman for 30 years when I first tried my hand at salmon fishing. I never actually wanted to, but a friend had been pestering me to join him and I finally ran out of excuses. He sweetened the deal by booking a splendid fishing lodge on the banks of the Scottish Dee, with space for both our families. Lots of food, good wine, bracing country walks – I was sure I could placate him with a couple of hours wielding the long rod.

I managed to borrow an old 14-foot Spey rod and some gear from my friend Doug, who winked knowingly and said, "And so you start on the road to penury." I smiled politely, but knew he was wrong. I was a trout fisherman, happiest stalking little upland streams with a wand of a rod and a pinch of tiny flies. Matching the hatch was my game, fooling a wily speckled quarry in its own realm. Salmon fishing was just lure fishing for posh people, wasn't it?

I think it took about 15 minutes to get utterly hooked. The ghillie was as sardonic and droll as I secretly hoped he would be. Keeping up a steady stream of abuse, he got me doing a double Spey cast of sorts within an hour and then left me to it. Amazingly, I actually hooked a salmon shortly after. A bad cast landed the line in a heap at the head of a pool. As it straightened out, the rod was almost ripped out of my hand. It was only on for a moment, throwing the hook as it thrashed on the surface, a great slab of angry silver. The sheer power was alien to me, in a different league to even the biggest trout I had caught. I stood there bewildered for a moment, as something took hold deep inside.

I booked to go back to the Dee the following year and joined a club near my home that had beats on the rivers Wye and Usk, probably the best UK salmon rivers outside of Scotland. I bought my own gear and had some proper casting lessons in the spring. I fished my club water at every opportunity, but didn't even see a salmon until June. My Dee trip was plagued by very low water, but at least I saw fish and even moved one to a Sunray Shadow fished across the tail of a pool late in the evening.

And so the trend continued. I tried other rivers in Scotland and further west in Wales, and carried on fishing my club beats, working out when it was worth a trip and when it was better to keep my powder dry. Even with my growing skills, it took three more years to register another mini success.

It was a gorgeous still evening in May. I was on the Wye, fishing on autopilot, with no hint that there was a single fish in the beat. I was just going through the motions, fishing a long-winged Monkey fly through the best run on the beat for the third time. Desperation tactics. Suddenly, a big silver salmon porpoised out of the water right next to me, and then another a bit further behind. I started stripping in my fly feverishly to recast when it stopped dead. "No!" I exclaimed. "A snag!"

But then the line started going thud, thud, thud. Perplexed, it took me a moment to realise that there was a fish on the end and it was shaking its head! I lifted the rod, the fish surged off and the line went slack. With my heart pounding, I immediately cast again, but the run was quiet once more. The pod had already moved through. A moment of sublime exhilaration in a desert of barren tedium.

Sometimes, the blanks were cruel. The following year, I fished the river Nith in October. The beat had been doing well and I forked out for a guide for three days to give myself the best chance. No drought this time, as rain fell steadily all day, the river slowly rising and discolouring. At 4pm, wet through and shivering, I finally gave up and left the guide to have a cast or two. He rewarded me by promptly hooking an 18lb hook-jawed beast – his biggest ever from the river. The next day was a washout; I learnt a different sort of lesson that day.

My eldest daughter tuned nine the following summer and I remembered that she had been two on that first Dee trip. Seven blank years, where did the time go? Time for a change of track. My favourite band, the Pixies, were headlining the Live At The Marquee music festival in Cork, Ireland in July and I wasn't going to miss it. Assuming that the famous Cork Blackwater was somewhere near Cork, I made some enquiries and received several hearty recommendations for Glenda Powell and her fishery. I had been reading the Blackwater fishing reports in Trout And Salmon for years. Something about the name was beguiling, as were the impressive annual catch statistics!

I was joined by my old friend Julian, who runs a traditional book bindery in London these days and does almost as much trout fishing as me. He likes the Scottish Highlands, where inexplicably he gets an annual invitation to fish with a member of parliament on a prized stretch of river. He had actually caught a couple of salmon by mistake the previous year when he was trying for trout.

I say 'friend', but if he did that again on this trip, he would be sleeping in the car. For once, the river was in perfect condition, the grilse run was in full swing and we had three long days to fish. Glenda was going to accompany us for the first day to show us the lies and hopefully help me to sharpen up my casting. In the end, she had to unteach all the bad habits I had learnt over seven years and soon I was casting better than I ever had. Jules was persuaded to put the trout rod down and have a go with the double hander. He turned out to be a natural – another strain on the friendship. We started upriver on the pretty Woodstream beat, but to be honest, the first session was mainly a casting lesson. We saw fish move, but none took pity on a couple of tyros.

After lunch, we moved down to Lower Kilmurry and the beautiful Lug Pool. Of all the stretches I had fished over the last seven years, this instantly became my favourite. Atmospheric, flattering and on this occasion, full of fish! They head and tailed out in the current and crashed out of the water in the deep eddy against the opposite bank. Most of them were grilse, the name given to salmon that have returned to the river after only one winter at sea, but some were big silver torpedoes that had obviously been feeding hard at sea for a number of years. There was no wind, I had found my casting mojo and we had our secret weapon advising us from the bank.

I went down first, a little self-tied Cascade on the business end. After a few casts, I found myself right in front of Glenda, who casually mentioned that I had reached the hot spot. Nothing on the first cast, but then she suggested a squarer one that would bring the fly across the lie with a bit more pace. Sure enough, after a few seconds the line moved away and a bright silver salmon leapt from the water with a flash of orange fly in its scissors.

I would like to say that I kept calm, followed Glenda's advice and it was just bad luck when it spat the hook after a minute. In reality, I panicked, held on for dear life and probably wrenched the fly from the poor fish's mouth. I wasn't distraught, quite the opposite. It was more success than I had ever had; I was concentrating hard and had been expecting a fish to take for the first time in my life. I can remember every detail.

Day two and Jules decided to fish for trout. We were upstream at Ballyhooly Bridge and had the beat to ourselves. We tackled up leisurely and then went our separate ways – Jules to the top end where we had seen trout rising and me down to the long run ending in a deep pool overhung with trees. No other anglers opposite; in fact, no humans in sight at all.

After a long private battle, a private victory would probably be fitting, and so it was. I worked my way down the run until I found myself facing a stepladder on the opposite bank. I don't know if it was my intuition, or if I subconsciously remembered something I had read on a forum once, but this felt like the prime place. Again, I tried a square cast and again, it worked. The fish took the same little Cascade and this time it stayed on. A grilse of about four pounds, but silver as a newly minted coin and most importantly, in my net. My first salmon.

I held it in the current for longer than necessary and then it slipped off into the dark water. What did I feel? Relief? Excitement? No, just a deep satisfaction and a feeling that I had reached another milestone on a lifelong salmon journey.

Day three we were back on Kilmurry, but this time we were alone and could have our choice of pools. I headed straight for the Island Stream and within 20 minutes, two more grilse had taken a liking to the little Cascade. What do they say about buses?

In the meantime, Jules had lost a good one in the Lug Pool and after commiserations and a tea break, I followed him down the Island Stream for a second time. With the downstream wind, he was throwing a lovely straight line with a left hand top double Spey, a cast I have never managed to master. You would never guess it was only his second day with a long rod, but he was about five feet short of the slack water on the other side of the current where the fish seemed to be taking.

With a slightly reckless single Spey, I was hitting the spot every third cast or so, and soon something bigger took hold. My rod bucked and bent like I had seen in all those YouTube videos, and my wrist was throbbing by the time it eventually slipped into the net. We didn't weigh it, but it had broad shoulders and a deep belly and I'm sure it would have tasted salty had I kissed it. A big grilse or a proper summer salmon? Who knows, I was over the moon.

I was genuinely shaky now. I lay in the grass at the top of the bank and watched Jules, willing a fish to take his fly. I didn't lend him my magic Cascade, though – I'm obviously not that generous. Then I caught a movement out of the corner of my eye, near the net that we had left where my fish was landed. A little flurry of black in the grass and then in the net. A mink, and then another one, scurrying all over, looking for the fishy meal that they could smell but not find. What a day this was turning out to be.

I would have been happy to stop there, but of course I carried on. We hadn't even fished Upper Kilmurry, so I headed up past the fishing hut to prospect in the stream on our side of the island. Overgrown and beyond my skills to fish from the bank, I slithered down into the water and waded precariously down the edge of what the old beat map told me was the Ghillie's' Pool. Well, that ghillie must have known something as the fly was snatched on the first cast by a grilse that shot out from behind the rock at the head of the pool. Number four for the day.

Further down, drunk with confidence, I flicked the fly under the overhanging branches on the island. A bigger fish took it this time, charging up and down the narrow pool, but never out of it, where I would have surely lost it. A seven-year stockpile of luck was finally being released. I netted it with my too-small folding net; long and lean and showing the colour of a fish that had been in the river a while.

I fished all the way down to the hut and by now, I was truly spent. Glenda and guests arrived for the evening session, beaming smiles and congratulations when they heard of my success. Mock modesty from me, I was thrilled with myself. Another cast and a pluck on the line. Surely not? But this fish fought strangely and came in easily and I soon saw why – it was a flounder! A miracle? Or perhaps a hallucination brought on by sensory overload? No, as Google told me later, quite normal for flounder to head up rivers, though it didn't mention a predilection for well-chewed Cascades.

Well, there you have it, seven years summarised in a few paragraphs. Is there a moral to this story? Did those seven barren years teach me anything about life and about myself? Of course not, I loved every minute and failure made the eventual success even sweeter. Although in retrospect, maybe I should have paid Glenda's Blackwater a visit a bit sooner. I surely will again.

22 WHAT WE DO IN THE SHALLOWS

I write this in the depths of winter, during yet another Covid lockdown. Everything is closed apart from supermarkets that sell the necessities of life. We can exercise outdoors once a day, but Rachel isn't even allowed to see her parents who live only a couple of miles away. Yet I am allowed to go fishing. Either there are a couple of mad keen anglers in the Tory cabinet, or there is a recognition that it is of great benefit to mental and physical health.

Unfortunately, there isn't much to catch in the middle of a frigid January. But I've been out nonetheless, roaming the banks of the little river near my house in the Somerset countryside, flicking a fly under the overhanging trees hoping for a perch or maybe a pike. There are even a few brown trout about, but it's closed season for them and they generally sulk in the depths when it gets this cold.

But it will be the first of March soon, when the trout and salmon season opens and the whole wonderful cycle starts again. Fishing in the early spring can be a frosty and hit and miss affair, but the potential rewards are great. The bigger resident fish have been left alone for a few months and are that bit less wary. April, May and June are the golden months though. The water warms up, aquatic insect life explodes, and the fish gorge themselves on chironomids, sedge, corixa, and the massive blooms of Daphnia – the tiny water flea.

The dry-fly fishing really takes off in the summer months as the fish look up for hatching nymphs and terrestrials blown onto the water. Hawthorn flies and Daddy Long Legs seem to be a particular favourite, or you may get lucky and be out fishing on that special day when the flying ants emerge and send the trout into a feeding frenzy. Even without the ants, on most soft overcast days in high summer you will see trout rising all day and it can all get a bit frenetic at dusk. Often, I'll still be casting frantically at moving fish when it is too dark to properly see at 10.30pm.

Autumn is my favourite time of year, as you get a bit of everything. The insect hatches pick up again as the water cools, but best of all, the millions of course fish fry and minnows start to congregate around any structure in the lakes. This may be your best chance of the year to get that huge trout or record perch. Unlike the early season when you are inching your flies through the depths, blindly searching for a lunker to tempt from its winter hibernation, autumn fishing is usually visual. The fish will be hunting in the surface layers, giving themselves away with bow waves, swirls or just 'nervous water' which is a wonderfully apt description for water that is being subtlety moved from below by unseen forces. A ripple going against the wind or even a flat spot in the waves that doesn't look quite normal could be your only clue to the presence of a roving fish.

By this time, the leaves are changing colours and it is starting to get a bit chilly. It is a last hurrah before the onset of winter and the start of yet another cycle. When I was growing up in Durban we didn't really have seasons. It was either very hot and rainy, or just hot and a bit rainy. I've grown to love the contrasts now, and it would just feel wrong to celebrate Christmas in the sweltering heat of mid-summer with a turkey on the braai, a concept which my kids find hilarious.

Kids – it seems like just last week that I was one myself and now I have two of them. Clever, funny, and very head strong girls, just like their mother. My teenage daughter even joins me fishing occasionally. She hasn't got the bug as badly as her dad, but she really enjoys it and has caught some lovely fish all on her own. Her first was actually on a dry fly, which made me question if she really is mine. My youngest is not so keen. She prefers animals to people and is very disapproving when we get the rods out.

If Covid allows, I'll hopefully get an Ireland trip in the autumn and I've got a pot of cash squirrelled away for a trip to Russia's Kola Peninsula at some point. Rachel is really keen to see Canada and who am I to disappoint her? I hear they have a fish or two. If travel restrictions mean I have to stay closer to home, then that is fine, too. Home is good.

I don't want to appear smug. It isn't all plain sailing. Having a safe haven is just one piece of the puzzle. Life is still full of ups and downs, challenges and stresses. Try being locked down for over a year with a teenage daughter and menopausal wife, and that will become very clear. It is important to have coping mechanisms and luckily, I have a brilliant one.

A question I get asked a lot by 'normal' people when they find out I am a fisherman is "Don't you get bored?" As if that is a bad thing. When do we get a chance to be bored in our hectic modern lives?

I don't, as it happens. With its constant challenges, puzzles and frustrations I can't say that I have the time for boredom when I am fishing. Even if the fish are being elusive, there is always something interesting going on at the water's edge. It doesn't have to be a giant condor overhead; it could be a curious mink, a theatrical mother duck protecting its brood, or even a single tiny insect struggling to break through the surface film to hatch, something you would never get to see if you weren't thigh deep in a lake.

I'll admit that on various points on the journey I have wondered exactly what it is that motivates me to endure all the hardships and mishaps just to catch a few trout. Maybe when I was younger, fishing was all about the thrill of the unknown – a gateway to adventure. An excuse to run off to remote and beautiful places that made my heart sing. I wasn't escaping anything; I had a fantastic childhood, but maybe it was a dose of the sailor's curse that compelled me to head out to discover what was over the horizon, or around the next bend in the river in my case.

As I grew older it has bordered on compulsion – tying flies that I knew I would never use, buying fly rods that I didn't really need and couldn't really afford. I let fishing hamper my career, sabotage my social life and scupper my love life, for seemingly no good reason. That is the funny thing about compulsions.

But maybe there is a reason after all. I've got another theory these days, although I may just be channelling that insufferable hippy student here, so bear with me for a minute. The human race has been evolving for millions of years. For millennia we were not just close to nature, we were nature. We lived off the land. We were prey for bears and lions. It has only been since the industrial revolution that we have become urbanised – just a blink of an eye in the course of human evolution. In that short time we have partitioned ourselves from the natural world, we do everything we can to vaccinate ourselves against its unpredictability and dangers. We control it and cage it and replace it with sterile concrete and manicured parks. Is that a good thing? Not to me it isn't. It can't be healthy to deny your true nature. We are just animals after all, hairless apes, although speaking for myself 'slightly less hairy apes' would be more accurate.

So where does fishing fit in? Apart from the beautiful wild places it takes us, maybe when a trout takes our fly it is validating us, making us part of the natural order of things that we are usually excluded from. I'm not one for guns, but I have a couple of friends that like shooting and will sit in a cold, damp hide for hours waiting for a duck to fly over. Their moment of ecstasy is the second they take the shot and the bird drops out of the sky, but they love the whole experience as they feel part of the landscape, not apart from it. I can understand that, and I do like a nice roast duck.

With my pragmatist's hat back on, it is probably all just down to simple brain chemicals, like the drive to eat and procreate. I have read that some extreme sports enthusiasts are actually addicted to the chemicals that their brains release when they jump out of planes or surf giant waves. They are quite literally adrenalin addicts.

I'm not comparing fishing with bungee jumping, but I'm sure brain chemicals play a part. The Japanese, for instance, extoll the virtues of shinrin-yoku for improving health and well-being. Shinrin is Japanese for "forest," and yoku means "to bath". So shinrin-yoku literally means 'forest bathing', though I gather that you keep your clothes on and don't actually get wet. It mostly involves doing something relaxing alone in the wilderness, much like fishing. Of course, being Japanese they have done scientific studies to validate the practice. One study compared two groups of subjects, one doing an activity in an urban location, and the other doing the exact same activity in a forest.

The forest group had significantly reduced pulse rates, increased levels of the chemicals associated with well-being and happiness, and decreased scores for depression, fatigue, anxiety, and confusion. I guess it is not just me then.

If you have read this far, you have probably gathered that I am not entirely of sound mind. I'm definitely harmless and I probably wouldn't do a pharmaceutical drug trial these days, but I am a bit prone to obsessive behaviour and a single mindedness that really annoys my dear wife. I have never dealt particularly well with stress, either, whether that be work, parenting demanding small children, or the financial worries that come with being an adult. I can't sleep, I become lethargic, and I feel like there is a weight permanently pressing down on my chest. If I don't return your phone call for a couple of weeks, then I am probably in one of these funks.

At these times, if I can escape for a few hours to a river or lake with a rod, I find that the stresses dissolve away. Fishing is like a soothing balm for my brain. Selecting a fly, the subconscious mechanics of making a good cast, absorbing and processing all the tiny clues in my surroundings that may help me fool a fish – maybe there is no space in my head for worries. It gives me a stillness that I don't get from anything else in life.

The older I get the more I realise that to be truly happy you can't just cruise along letting life just happen to you. You have to actively build a life and a home where happiness becomes your natural state. Everyone is different, but for me that includes being immersed in nature and near water as much as possible, and surrounding myself with like-minded folk. Where once fishing was all-consuming, now it is just a few stitches in life's rich tapestry as my old man would say… and this feral fisherman is rather happy with his tapestry so far.

I'll leave you with a thought from the American naturalist and philosopher Henry David Thoreau, who once said "Many men go fishing all of their lives without knowing that it is not fish they are after". Unhelpfully, he didn't go on to say what they are actually after. But maybe that is up to us as individuals to find out.

A golden start to a fishing life.
The author aged 17.
Photo by Mark Hewat

Lock up your daughters - in case they get jealous of our hair. Author and Julian aged 20 and dressed for success.

Releasing a rainbow on a remote river near Coyhaique in Chile.
Photo by Joyce Norman

Inhospitable even to foot fungi - a sulphurous lake high in the Bolivian Andes.

A big salt flat, or a tiny truck? Salar de Uyuni, Bolivia.

A feral fisherman in his native habitat.
Lake Rotoiti, South Island, New Zealand.
Photo by Mark Hewat

Mark Hewat coaxing a good fish away from the undercut bank on a small South Island stream.
Photo by author.

Mark Hewat bites the bear, again.
Photo by author.

On the path to Blagdon Lake,
Somerset, England.
Photo by author.

Withnail and couple of fine Scottish
browners that I wish I had caught.
Photo by Julian Pendlebury.

Alan nets yet another Chew Valley lump.
Photo by author.

A Chew Valley Lake pike taken on a foam Daddy Long Legs 'dibbled' across the surface in the autumn. The lake record is almost three times the size.
Photo by Alan Shearn.

A salmon at last.
Photo by Julian Pendlebury

Home is good. Sunrise on a local Somerset lake.
Photo by author.

ABOUT THE AUTHOR

After many years as a roaming trout bum, Dave is now settled in the North Somerset countryside with his wife and two daughters. He writes 'technical stuff' for a living and about fishing for the love of it, even though by his own admission he is an enthusiastic rather than skilled fisherman.

He likes cider and cows, and his kids apparently sound like pirates.

Thanks

A special thanks to my friend Owen Bailey who is a proper writer and helped me with proofreading, editing and many other things that I am clueless about.

Thanks to Trevor Furness and Anthony Durnford who ran the fishing clubs at my junior and senior schools, and who were both instrumental in helping me at the start of my fly-fishing journey. They truly had the patience of saints.

Thanks to Mark, Doug and Alan for their friendship and guidance on the Bristol lakes when I was first starting out.

Thanks to Julian and Dr Mark for their friendship over many years and for letting me use their excellent photographs for free.

And finally, thanks to my wife Rachel for seeing something in that quirky, lost South African that she first met on Putney Bridge on 31st December 1999.

Printed in Poland
by Amazon Fulfillment
Poland Sp. z o.o., Wrocław

85940173R00091